THE UNITED NATIONS
GENOCIDE CONVENTION

SAMUEL TOTTEN AND HENRY THERIAULT

THE
UNITED NATIONS
GENOCIDE
CONVENTION
AN INTRODUCTION

UNIVERSITY OF TORONTO PRESS

Toronto Buffalo London

© University of Toronto Press 2020
Toronto Buffalo London
utorontopress.com
Printed in Canada

ISBN 978-1-4875-0606-3 (cloth)   ISBN 978-1-4875-3322-9 (ePUB)
ISBN 978-1-4875-2408-1 (paper)   ISBN 978-1-4875-3321-2 (PDF)

Library and Archives Canada Cataloguing in Publication

Title: The United Nations Genocide Convention: An introduction / Samuel Totten,
    Henry Theriault.
Names: Totten, Samuel, author. | Theriault, Henry, author.
Description: Includes bibliographical references and index.
Identifiers: Canadiana 20190181591 | ISBN 9781487506063 (cloth) |
    ISBN 9781487524081 (paper)
Subjects: LCSH: Convention on the Prevention and Punishment of the Crime
    of Genocide (1948 December 9) | LCSH: Genocide—Law and legislation. |
    LCSH: Genocide—Case studies. | LCGFT: Case studies.
Classification: LCC KZ7180.A61948 T68 2020 | DDC 345/.0251—dc23

We welcome comments and suggestions regarding any aspect of our publications— please feel free to contact us at news@utorontopress.com or visit us at utorontopress.com.

Every effort has been made to contact copyright holders; in the event of an error or omission, please notify the publisher.

University of Toronto Press acknowledges the financial assistance to its publishing program of the Canada Council for the Arts and the Ontario Arts Council, an agency of the Government of Ontario.

Canada Council
for the Arts

Conseil des Arts
du Canada

ONTARIO ARTS COUNCIL
CONSEIL DES ARTS DE L'ONTARIO
an Ontario government agency
un organisme du gouvernement de l'Ontario

MIX
Paper from
responsible sources
FSC
www.fsc.org   FSC® C103567

Contents

Acknowledgments

I wish to sincerely thank Ms Natalie Fingerhut, History Editor at the University of Toronto Press, for her interest and support of this project/ book, and her incredible support and assistance throughout the project. To assert that I enjoy working with her is an understatement. I love working with her.

I also wish to thank the external reviewers for their thoughtful and valuable feedback of the book proposal. Many of the comments and insights proved extremely helpful in revising and refining aspects for the project.

S.T.

Any work on genocide should start with recognition of the many victims who have died and survived over the years, centuries, and millennia of genocide. The work of genocide scholars bears witness to their suffering and is a commitment to prevent such suffering in the future.

Specific authors are of course just the "tip of the iceberg." Whatever any of us does depends on foundations laid by previous thinkers in our fields and beyond and would not be possible without continuing discussions and debates with other scholars. Of course, the responsibility for shortcomings is entirely the individual author's. With this in mind, I wish to recognize founders of the field of genocide studies, beginning with Raphael Lemkin and continuing through the founders of the International Association of Genocide Studies (IAGS), Helen Fein, Israel Charny, Roger Smith, and Robert Melson. Being able to read their work and participate in conferences, editorial boards, and other activities with them and other scholars has been invaluable for my development as a scholar. I would like to extend that gratitude to the many members of IAGS and other associations and organizations whose work and personal commitment to ending genocide has inspired me and given me crucial tools for understanding and responding to the "odious scourge." I especially wish to acknowledge my colleagues on the Executive and Advisory Boards of IAGS, Adam Muller, Melanie O'Brien, Ami Fagin, Stephanie Wolfe, Kerry Whigham, Timothy Williams, Sara Elise Brown, Christian Gudehus, Hollie Nyseth Brehm, Hilary Earl, Suren Manukyan, Andrew Woolford, and, more recently, Armen Marsoobian, Emily Sample, and Caroline Bennett for doing so much work and making so many impressive sacrifices to create an environment in which serious study of genocide has been possible. Richard Hovannisian, Antranig Kasbarian, Dikran Kaligian, George Aghjayan, Khatchig Mouradian, Peter Balakian, Bilgin Ayata, Debórah Dwork, Joyce Apsel, Uğur Üngör, Taner Akçam, and Jermaine McCalpin have offered me so much through their work and collegiality. I have had the privilege of great ongoing conversations about genocide issues with co-editors and others at *Genocide Studies International* and *Genocide Studies and Prevention*, including George Shirinian, Greg Sarkissian, Maureen Hiebert, Nick Robins, Alex Alvarez, Elisa von Joeden-Forgey, the late Herb Hirsch, and of course Sam Totten. My university has been a tremendous support as well, beginning with colleagues from my years in the Philosophy Department, Daniel Shartin, Kristin Waters, Jerry Robbins, Courtney Schlosser, Richard Schmitt, José Mendoza, and Elena Cuffari. I cannot thank Dan and Kris enough for the myriad ways they have mentored and supported me over the years. I hesitate to extend this list beyond my old department, as I would have to list hundreds of faculty and staff members past and present. Suffice it to say that Worcester State University has been an amazing home for me for more than two decades, providing me with wondrously insightful and politically committed colleagues across academic departments and administrative offices. I would, however, be remiss if I did not at least mention Provost Lois Wims; Deans Linda Larrivee, Russ Pottle, and Bobbi Kyle; Nathalie Torres-Serrano, Noah Dion, and Sarah Strout for fostering an exceptionally positive team atmosphere in Academic Affairs these past two years that has provided a wonderful foundation for continued intellectual growth, as well as Linda Donahue of our library, who has been invaluable in helping me access key books. I end with thanks to my mentor and friend, the late philosopher Robert John Ackermann, of whose work mine is but a poor, inadequate extension.

For this book in particular, the folks at UTP have been exceptional to work with, especially Natalie Fingerhut and Christine Robertson. It is not a stretch to say that great editing as they have done has been essential to the shaping of this book, which would not exist without them. Our three reviewers provided valuable suggestions and challenges that improved the book immeasurably—I only wish I could thank them by name.

H.T.

Introduction

The express purpose of *The United Nations Genocide Convention: An Introduction* is to provide students (primarily undergraduates and Master's candidates) across the globe with a comprehensive, detailed, and relatively easy to understand text, along with the means to help them become thoroughly knowledgeable about—and conversant with—the unique wording and key components of the United Nations Convention on the Prevention and Punishment of the Crime of Genocide (hereafter UNCG) and particularly the definition of "genocide" found therein. At the same time, we have set out to produce an accessible text while not shying away from presenting the various complexities and ambiguities of the UNCG.

As longtime scholars of genocide, we firmly believe that it is essential for anyone who plans to speak about, study, analyze, discuss, debate, and/ or report on a case of genocide to thoroughly understand the UNCG and its definition of genocide. The UNCG, for the time being at least, is the document that scholars, state governments, UN officials, and international jurists use to ascertain whether a particular conflict constitutes genocide or not. In fact, the UNCG is the legal standard that prosecutors, defense attorneys, and judges use to issue warrants on charges of genocide, try alleged cases of genocide, and make judgments about the guilt or innocence of those on trial for genocide. This was the case at both the International Criminal Tribunal for Rwanda (ICTR) and the International Criminal Tribunal for the Former Yugoslavia (ICTY), and remains true at the International Criminal Court

(ICC). It is for these reasons and more that UNCG constitutes a crucial foundation in the study and understanding of genocide.

We, the authors, appreciate the complexities inherent in various aspects of the UNCG, including the definition of genocide. Indeed, we, ourselves, have wrestled with many of the complexities over the years, particularly in attempting to comprehend the ways in which various actors (prosecutors, defense lawyers, judges, as well as political figures) at the ICTR, ICTY, ICC, and beyond have understood or misunderstood key aspects of the UNCG.

Over the years, we have also watched and listened, often aghast, as various government officials, journalists, and certain scholars, among others, in the United States and elsewhere, have embarrassingly misinterpreted the concept of genocide and/or apparently purposely misled the general populace as to that which constitutes genocide. In the face of ongoing atrocity crimes (e.g., in the former Yugoslavia, Rwanda, and Darfur, Sudan, to name but three instances), certain high-level officials (e.g., at the UN and in the US government) and the international media, among others, have repeatedly miscast various mass killings—in certain cases referring to genocidal actions as civil wars, crimes against humanity, war crimes, and/or ethnic cleansing, or vice versa. Sometimes such misinterpretation of the UNCG resulted from ignorance and/or misunderstanding of key aspects of it (including, for example, legal terms). In such cases, officials were culpable for failing to exercise their due diligence prior to issuing an assertion, opinion, and/or statement, which ended up being inaccurate as a result. In other cases, though, the misrepresentations were more calculated. Some officials either purposely misapplied the UNCG or purposely avoided mentioning the term "genocide," implicitly suggesting that they had looked at the UNCG and had come to the decision that the killings they were addressing failed to rise to the level of genocide. In other words, officials *purposely* misinterpreted the UNCG in order to support their governments' or some other entity's position in regard to whether ongoing atrocity crimes constituted genocide or not.

More than once, such instances have resulted in allowing the killing to continue unabated. How many deaths resulted from such unprofessional, if not immoral, actions, no one can say for sure. But in one case—that of the 1994 genocide in Rwanda—it is well-documented that at various points during the genocide some eight to ten thousand people were being murdered every day. For weeks on end during that period, officials in the administration of US President Bill Clinton were ordered not to use the term "genocide" to describe what was taking place in Rwanda (Jehl 1994, para. 1). Similar avoidance among representatives on the UN Security Council, in the view of many experts, led to maladroit decisions that likely cost tens of thousands—if not hundreds of thousands—of lives.

With this in mind, the second goal of this book is to present readers with a framework for understanding and evaluating both past and new outbreaks of mass atrocities across the globe. This might include, for example, cases that are still controversially denied, such as the Ottoman Turkish genocide of Christian minorities (1915–23), or relatively recent cases in which new knowledge continues to be uncovered. These newer cases include the ongoing crisis in Myanmar, where radical Buddhists and state army troops have sporadically killed members of the Rohingya in Rakhine State, destroyed one Rohingya village after another, and forced hundreds of thousands from their homes and country, with most Rohingya having fled to roughshod refugee camps in Bangladesh.

Unsurprisingly, aside from scholars and certain well-read others, when most people are asked to define "genocide" in their own words, many, if not most, respond with a single word or a simple phrase, which they believe captures the essence of the term and concept behind it (e.g., "massacre," "slaughter," "extermination," "annihilation," or "bloodbath"). Given the role of public opinion in driving or preventing intervention against genocide, it is critical that the public be well-informed regarding the concept of genocide. The same is true in regard to international and national leaders and the media, among others. A simplistic understanding of such a complex issue is more than a little unsatisfactory.

Among the many issues that readers will be introduced to in this book are:

♦ The conceptual innovations and legal ramifications of the tireless efforts of Raphael Lemkin to establish the UNCG as international law.
♦ The drafting of the UNCG and the debates that ensued over which kinds of groups were to be protected under the UNCG and which were not.
♦ The various compromises that were made during the drafting process of the UNCG and the effect that had in regard to, for example, which types of groups were and were not to be afforded protection under the UNCG.
♦ The specific wording found in Article II of the UNCG and a clear and accurate delineation of what the words mean.
♦ Key legal terms used by international law experts when discussing the issue of genocide and what these terms mean in layperson's language.
♦ The components that must be evident for a case of atrocity crimes to constitute genocide.

+ The major distinctions between genocide, crimes against humanity, war crimes, and ethnic cleansing.
+ Real-world applications of the UNCG.
+ The role of the UNCG in the prosecution of genocide.

That is a lot to address in a relatively short book, but it is necessary in order to provide readers with the understanding they will need in order to begin to thoroughly understand the concept and issue of genocide.

While we provide in-depth information about the UNCG in the most readable fashion possible, we appreciate that many points are not easily understood during a first reading. Therefore, we recommend the following approach to enhance a reader's understanding of various points and issues herein. Plan on reading each section of the chapter two or three times. The first time around, read the section just to get a feel for what is being said. In doing so, look up any words that are unfamiliar. The second time around, identify and note the most important points. Look up any events, incidents, and so on, that you feel a need to know more about. The third time around (if even needed), highlight the key points, and rewrite them in your own words. Hopefully, this process will provide each reader with a solid understanding of the various issues, help make the information less imposing and/or confusing, and equip readers to more confidently discuss the issues with others.

Readers who engage the full range of issues raised in this book may wish to go into greater depth than is possible in an introductory text. In order to construct as accessible a text as possible, we have designed the book to be an entry path into further study of genocide in its legal, historical, political, and philosophical dimensions, but without privileging any specific discipline in our treatment. To do otherwise would have meant focusing on one set of issues in depth while ignoring others, which would have undermined the purpose of providing a general introduction to the UNCG, along with a foundation for further, more specialized study. The detailed annotated bibliography at the conclusion of the book offers students suggested avenues for more advanced study of the UNCG.

We truly believe that the more people are conversant with all facets of genocide—beginning with the UNCG—the more likely it will be that someday, some way, there will be an effective and successful movement towards the prevention of what some have deemed "the crime of crimes." We welcome you, the reader, to join the growing but still exclusive coterie of individuals who are truly well-informed about complexities of the

UNCG and the role that it plays—or, at least, should play—in attempting to ascertain whether a particular case constitutes genocide or not, the issuance of warrants in regard to alleged cases of genocide, and the undertaking of trials in which genocide has allegedly been committed, including the complex task of finding defendants innocent or guilty vis-à-vis the crime of genocide.

References

Jehl, Douglas. 1994. "Officials Told to Avoid Calling Rwanda Killings 'Genocide.'" *The New York Times*, June 10, 1994. https://www.nytimes.com/1994/06/10 /world/officials-told-to-avoid-calling-rwanda-killings-genocide.html
United Nations General Assembly. 1948. *Convention on the Prevention and Punishment of the Crime of Genocide*. December 9. United Nations Treaty Series, vol. 78, p. 277 (A/RES/260). New York: United Nations.

1 Raphael Lemkin: The Man Who Coined the Term "Genocide" and His Indefatigable Effort in the Development and Ratification of the UNCG

Ever since the end of World War II, the term and concept of "genocide" has become increasingly familiar to and used by people across the globe. Today, it is so universally known that it is used in newspapers, political discussions, Hollywood movies, and even in the lyrics of popular music.

However, like other relatively recent yet now ubiquitous terms such as "email" and "the internet," the word itself is quite new. In fact, it has only existed since the early 1940s. It is rather astounding that in such a short period of time it has become a part of virtually every language and is commonly used by journalists, activists, and educators at various levels of schooling.

While many new words evolve organically within a language, it is often difficult to determine their origins. That is not the case with "genocide"; rather, we can point not only to its first published use but also to the person who developed the word and the exact process he followed.

What is also striking about the development of the concept of "genocide" is that it was not just a vocabulary exercise. On the contrary, it resulted from the decades-long attempt by Raphael Lemkin to internationally outlaw genocide. Coining the term was part of Lemkin's strategy to outlaw genocide, which was a phenomenon he had found to have occurred throughout recorded human history.

In most cases, it is inaccurate to focus on a single individual as the key to a great historical change. Even Susan B. Anthony, Mahatma Gandhi, Eleanor Roosevelt, Martin Luther King Jr, and Nelson Mandela, who have been credited with making profoundly significant changes in society, were

1

part of massive movements of people who were pushing for such change. As much as they led various movements and the process of change, they were also products of their times and the beneficiaries of earlier efforts vis-à-vis the issues they struggled for or struggled against. Raphael Lemkin is a stark contrast in this regard.

While Lemkin was not without predecessors—for instance, in the eighteenth century, as Lemkin was aware, Genevan philosopher Jean-Jacques Rousseau argued that the mass killing of civilians of a country that had been defeated in war was a human rights violation and morally wrong—such influences were few. In Lemkin's case, he conceived of "genocide," and then fought indefatigably for its recognition as an international crime. Lemkin's role regarding the UNCG is so unique, so profound, and so central that there is no way to discuss the development of the UNCG without focusing on the life of Raphael Lemkin. We leave it to the reader to ponder the implication that the man who goaded humanity to recognize genocide for what it is and to outlaw it is much less well-known than major perpetrators of genocide such as Hitler, Goebbels, Himmler, and even Pol Pot, Slobodan Milošević, and Omar al-Bashir.

Raphael Lemkin (24 June 1900–28 August 1959) has been referred to as "the Father of the Genocide Convention," "the Man Who Criminalized Genocide," and a "One-Man NGO" (nongovernmental organization). He not only created the concept and coined the term "genocide" but was also instrumental in prodding the international community to establish the United Nations Convention on the Prevention and Punishment of the Crime of Genocide (UNCG). Lemkin was obsessed with the need to establish such a convention, and as he went about doing so, it was obvious that he was a man on a mission. More than a few people, in fact, perceived Lemkin as a pest, in that he cajoled and harangued anyone and everyone (e.g., United Nations officials as well as officials representing their respective nations in the development of the UNCG) who was part of the drafting process in an attempt to prod them to incorporate his unique insights and ideas into the Convention.

Just who was this man with such an obsession? Lemkin was born into an upper-middle-class Jewish family on a large farm in Bezwondene, Poland, which was, at the time, located in imperial Russia.[1] His father was a farmer, while his mother was a painter, a philosopher, and a linguist. His mother homeschooled Lemkin and his two brothers, as she firmly believed that "young children should first of all be indoctrinated in feelings and sensitivities, [as] the great impact of early emotions [formed] the character" (Cooper

2008, 9). Speaking of what he learned at his mother's knee as she taught him and his two brothers songs and poetry by Siemlon Nadson, Lemkin (2002) made the following observation:

> As I [try] to reconstruct the content of these sonnet-songs, the following picture of the world appears from them. There is much evil on earth and there is much injustice. The innocent and the poor suffer. They are often murdered in cold blood.... The poor and the innocent must be helped.... The songs offered hope for a betterment of the world, for the cessation of evil, for the protection of the weak. The appeal for the protection of the innocent from destruction set a chain reaction in my mind. It followed me all my life. (369–70)

Lemkin further commented that the stories and themes of such songs and poetry spurred him to voraciously read books about the persecution and destruction of religious, racial, and other minority groups.

By a relatively young age, around fourteen years old, Lemkin was capable of reading, writing, and speaking Hebrew, Russian, Ukrainian, and Yiddish. These were in addition to Polish, his native language. Later in life, he learned to read, write, and speak English, French, German, and Swedish. Some have claimed that Lemkin spoke nine languages and was able to read fourteen (Sayapin 2009, 1157).

As a result of growing up in Poland during the first two decades of the twentieth century, Lemkin and his family frequently heard about anti-Jewish violence. And what he heard was frightening: "News of a pogrom in the city of Bialystok, fifty miles away, came to our farm. The mobs opened the stomachs of their victims and stuffed them with the feathers from pillows and feather comforters" (Lemkin 2002, 370).

The suppression of Jewish people's rights, the hatred spewed against them in propaganda, and the violence aimed at them were common in Eastern Europe at the time. So was the fact that the agitators and perpetrators of such vitriol and violence were generally not held accountable for their actions. The latter was due to the fact that legal authorities looked the other way when marginalized groups were persecuted. Lemkin's world seems to have reflected what he read in the works he studied.

According to his autobiography, when he was twelve years old, Lemkin read *Quo Vadis*, a novel by Henryk Sienkiewicz, which was about the persecution of Christians in Rome by Nero (37–68 CE). Lemkin found what he read about Nero and Rome's treatment of the Christians extremely upsetting. Indeed, reading *Quo Vadis* was a seminal event in Lemkin's life in that it drew his attention to an important, violent aspect of human history.

As Lemkin (2002) said about his reading of *Quo Vadis*: "Here was a group of people collectively sentenced to death [solely because] they believed in Christ. And nobody could help them. I became so fascinated with the story that I looked up all the similar instances in history ..." (365). From the beginning, then, Lemkin understood that what concerned him was a problem not just of one or a few groups, but a kind of violence that had occurred many times throughout history.

At the age of fifteen, Lemkin read about the mass killing (now deemed a genocide) of the Armenian people by the Ottoman Turks which began in 1915. This caused him immense distress; in fact, it was something that he carried with him to the day he died. As a teenager, he simply could not understand how members of one group could kill members of another primarily because the targeted population (i.e., the victims) belonged to a different group. He was just as baffled as to why those responsible for the killing of the Armenians did so with impunity. In this regard, he later said:

> In Turkey, more than 1,200,000 Armenians were put to death.... After the end of the war, some 150 Turkish war criminals were arrested and interned by the British Government.... Then one day I read in the newspaper that all Turkish war criminals were to be released. I was shocked. A nation was killed and the guilty persons were set free. Why is a man punished when he kills another man? *Why is the killing of a million a lesser crime than the killing of a single individual?* (Lemkin 2002, 371; emphasis added)

Slowly but surely, all of the aforementioned issues (the mistreatment of the Jews, the murder of the Christians by Nero, and the destruction of the Armenians by the Ottoman Turks, as well as other major cases of mass killing) contributed to Lemkin's ever-increasing concern that perpetrators of such horrific atrocities never seemed to be held accountable for the violence they committed.

At the age of fourteen or fifteen, Lemkin entered his first formal school setting. At that time, he matriculated at the University of Lwów, where he studied philosophy and philology. Ultimately, he decided to study law, and went on to earn a doctorate at the University of Heidelberg in Germany.

In 1921, while studying law in Germany, Lemkin became engrossed in the trial of Soghomon Tehlirian, a young Armenian, who, Lemkin had read, witnessed the murder of his entire family by the Ottoman Turks and in retaliation had shot and killed Talaat Pasha, a chief architect of the Armenian genocide, on a Berlin street. This, too, would have a profound influence on his future work.

Concerning his studies, and in particular international law, Lemkin (2002) made the following observation:

> I studied law, I became interested in a special field of international law, namely, international criminal law, which is quite a narrow subject, highly technical. I felt that if the killing of one man was a crime, and is not a matter of negotiations between the guilty and policemen, the destruction of millions of people should also be a crime, and, moreover, it should be an international crime to the effect that the guilty, whether heads of states or private individuals, would be held responsible as criminals. Killing of nations is not a political matter that permits interpretations and negotiations. (367)

Upon graduation with his doctorate, Lemkin taught for a year. Then, from 1929 to 1934, he went to work in the public prosecutor's office in Warsaw. During roughly that same period (1929–35), Lemkin served as the secretary for the Committee for Codification of the Laws of the Polish Republic.

In 1933, outraged over the persecution and massacre of Assyrians in Iraq, Lemkin crafted a paper on what he referred to as "barbarity" and "vandalism" (essentially, mass slaughter and cultural destruction, respectively). In tracing Lemkin's influence on the UNCG, it is important to recognize that, according to the Convention, cultural destruction in the absence of physical destruction is *not* genocide. "Cultural genocide" is typically understood to mean eliminating facets of a group's culture to such an extent that the group is no longer able to hold on to its identity, and thus dissolves as an identity group. This could include outlawing use of its language, preventing members from practicing its characteristic religion, and so on. While Lemkin and many subsequent scholars have viewed cultural genocide as a form of genocide, it was, as just noted, excluded from the UNCG in the drafting process. Similarly, "ethnocide" is often used as an equivalent of "cultural genocide," and thus is excluded from coverage by the UNCG as well. The point is: the focus on physical destruction is clear in the wording of Article II of the UNCG.[2]

Lemkin submitted the aforementioned paper, which was a proposal to outlaw "barbarism" and "vandalism" (Lemkin 2019, para. 3), to the 1933 Fifth Conference for the Unification of Penal Law in Madrid, Spain, held in conjunction with the Fifth Committee of the League of Nations (Lemkin 1933, paras. 12–24; Lemkin 1944, 91). As Lemkin prepared to leave for Spain to present his paper, he received a late-night telephone call from a justice on the Polish Supreme Court, who was to serve as the chief Polish delegate at the League of Nations conference. The justice, with great embarrassment, informed Lemkin that the Polish Minister of Justice was against Lemkin's attendance at the conference. Lemkin goes on to note that the caller also mentioned that news articles had appeared in the anti-Semitic but influential newspaper *Gazeta Warszawska*, in which Lemkin's proposal was attacked. In part, the articles charged Lemkin was "acting solely for the protection of [his] own race" (Lemkin 2002, 373). In turn, Nazi representatives at the League of Nations meeting in Madrid mocked the thrust of Lemkin's proposal.

During this same period of time, Lemkin traveled throughout Europe with the purpose of informing the leaders of various states about the nature of his proposal, and to urge them to join his campaign "to make an international crime the destruction of national, racial or religious groups" (Lemkin 2002, 367). As a result of his campaign, he dolefully commented, "Cold water was poured on me, and I was urged not to go on with fantastic predictions and with the formulation of laws which are not necessary, because they apply to crime[s] which occur seldom in history" (367).

The above events served as the genesis and foundational efforts of Lemkin's determination and lifelong pursuit of a legal means to prevent mass atrocity crimes and to punish their perpetrators.

Ultimately, due to anti-Semitism and the fact that the Polish state was intent on appeasing the Nazis, it was made known that Lemkin could no longer remain in his position with the public prosecutor's office, and he resigned in 1934. From there, Lemkin went into the private practice of law and taught at a local university until World War II broke out and the Germans attacked Warsaw. During the attack, his home, his office, and the institution where he taught were all either damaged or outright destroyed.

Lemkin decided to flee the Nazi onslaught. Try as he might, Lemkin failed to convince his family to flee Poland with him. Ultimately, Lemkin managed to reach Lithuania on his way to Sweden.

Lemkin landed a position as a lecturer at the University of Stockholm. While in Sweden, he engaged in a detailed study of Nazi jurisprudence and Germany's occupation of Europe. The product of these efforts was ultimately published in November 1944 in a book entitled *Axis Rule in Occupied Europe*. It was in this book that the term "genocide" appeared in print for the first time, and where Lemkin explained that he created the term by combining the Greek prefix "genos," meaning "race-," and the Latin suffix "-cide," meaning "killing." James Fussell (2003) has noted that Lemkin "felt this word [genocide] was very appropriate because it had a moral force because of its parallel with the word 'homicide,' [and] it was a word for destruction which could only be applied to human groups" (para. 47). Lemkin "immediately began warning whoever would listen about Nazi Germany's plans for the 'Final Solution'" (United States Holocaust Memorial Museum 2013, para. 48).

In 1941, upon receiving an invitation to teach at Duke University Law School in North Carolina, Lemkin left Europe for the United States. During World War II, Lemkin also served as a legal adviser at the War Department (Winter 2013, para. 12). Still later, Lemkin taught law at Yale University Law School.

Only Lemkin and his brother Elias survived the Holocaust. All of the rest of his family members, some forty-nine people, met their deaths at the hands of the Nazis. His parents were gassed in the Treblinka extermination camp (Winter 2013, para. 5). One can only begin to attempt to imagine the psychological toll such loss had on Lemkin, and yet he continued apace in his determination and efforts to incorporate the criminalization of genocide as a special and unique crime into international law.

At the conclusion of World War II in 1945, Lemkin traveled to Nuremberg, Germany, where he served as an adviser to United States Justice Robert Jackson at the International Military Tribunal at Nuremberg,[3] and "persuaded the Allied prosecutors to add genocide to the bill of indictment against the Nazi high command" (Winter 2013, para. 14). Ultimately, though, when the various Nazi leaders were tried for their alleged crimes at the Nuremberg Trials, they were not charged with genocide. Rather, they were charged and tried on one or more of the following charges: war crimes, crimes against peace, and crimes against humanity. Explaining this turn of events, Lemkin (2002) stated, "The Tribunal declared that it is bound by the Statute of the International Military Tribunal, which did not contain the charge of genocide" (385).[4]

Firm in his belief that genocide was something altogether different from the aforementioned crimes, indeed, something profoundly distinct and graver, Lemkin argued that it was imperative to include genocide as a specific crime under international law. Lemkin fought to make that a reality. In doing so, he focused on that goal to the exclusion of all others, working day and night for years on end.

Between 1945 and 1948, Lemkin moved between New York City, Geneva, and Paris, all of which were locales where the UN Charter and the UNCG were being pounded out. Lemkin drafted and presented the first iteration of a Convention on the Prevention and Punishment of the Crime of Genocide to the Paris Peace Conference in 1945. To his dismay, his proposal failed to attract the support it needed to move forward.

Typifying Lemkin's tenacity and dedication, he began a major lobbying effort to convince various international actors to support his idea. As noted above, Lemkin spoke to anyone and everyone with potential influence about the concept of genocide and the critical need to make it a crime in international law. It didn't matter what the occasion or location was—public meetings, private meetings, the offices of officials, the corridors of conferences, receptions, lounge areas, the lobbies of hotels, or press conferences— Lemkin addressed the issue about which he was obsessed. And he did not simply speak to a person once and leave it at that, but approached the same individual over and over again.

Due to Lemkin's relentless efforts, a resolution supporting the consideration of an international convention on genocide was eventually put before the United Nations, and the resolution was approved in November 1946. For the next two years, a host of committees worked on and revised drafts of the Convention, high-level officials of various nations commented on the drafts, several states added amendments to particular drafts, and some states even wrote up and submitted alternative texts. Throughout the process, the drafts, comments, amendments, and alternative texts were discussed, debated, and/ or revised, with each change reflecting, at least to a certain extent, various states' perspectives, concerns, and desires—many of which were greatly influenced by a state's history vis-à-vis its treatment of its own people and others. During this period, Lemkin served as an adviser to the effort. Remarkably, "the Ad Hoc Committee [tasked with drafting the UNCG] met a total of twenty-eight times over the course of April and May 1948, preparing a new draft convention and an accompanying commentary" (Schabas 2009, 70).

Early on, it became obvious to Lemkin that, even though he was the progenitor behind the advent of the UNCG, he was going to have to be open to compromise, and accept a final document that included some aspects he did not favor. More specifically, at the point when it became apparent that certain states wished to include "political groups" as one of the groups protected under the UNCG, Lemkin capitulated even though he was against this, for he believed there were more important issues to take a hard stand on. Lemkin was against the inclusion of political groups because he said they "lacked the required permanency" (Schabas 2009, 61). In other words, a person of a particular race could not change his/her/their race, whereas one, for example, who was a Republican in the United States could certainly change over to being a Democrat.

Ultimately, "political groups" were removed as one of the protected groups due to the demands of, among others, both the Soviet Union and Poland. The

Soviet Union desired the exclusion of political groups due to its actions against purported political foes during the Great Terror (1936–38) and beyond.

As discussed above, while Lemkin was in favor of including "cultural genocide"—"the destruction 'by brutal means of the specific characteristics of the human group, that is to say, its moral and sociological characteristics'" (Schabas 2009, 174)—in the Convention, it was eventually excluded. Lemkin's concept of genocide was not limited to the physical destruction of groups through mass killing and other measures (e.g., the introduction of disease) meant to result in mass deaths; rather, he saw genocide fundamentally as the destruction of the viability of the group, and this could include measures that would leave most if not all members alive but stripped of their group identity and thus forced to assimilate into the perpetrator group. Cultural genocide was therefore an important concept for him.

Early in the drafting process, the United States was adamantly against the inclusion of cultural genocide, while France was less adamant but still did not support inclusion of the concept. Ultimately, the Secretariat "cautioned the [UN] General Assembly about covering too much ground with the Convention, insisting upon a restrictive definition: '[O]therwise there is a danger of the idea of genocide being expanded indefinitely to include the law of war, the rights of peoples to self-determination, the protection of minorities, the respect of human rights, etc.'" (quoted in Schabas 2009, 174). This concern has been a mainstay in academic debates over the definition of genocide to the present day. Tellingly, though, even in the more limited form of the UNCG, genocide still goes beyond simple mass killing.

Finally, on 9 December 1948, the Convention on the Prevention and Punishment of the Crime of Genocide was adopted unanimously by the United Nations General Assembly. Notably, it was the first human rights treaty passed by the UN General Assembly. (The very next day the Universal Declaration of Human Rights was also adopted by the UN General Assembly.) While Lemkin found great satisfaction in this, he knew his work was far from over. Now he needed to lobby all nations possible to ratify the UNCG, which he did, relentlessly.

To become law, the UNCG had to be ratified by at least twenty member states of the UN. Lemkin pushed himself beyond exhaustion to get the UNCG ratified, ultimately ending up with four more signatories than were needed. In 1951, the UNCG became international law. But there were a number of holdouts, including but not limited to the Soviet Union, Great Britain, and the United States, which, respectively, ratified the UNCG in 1954, 1970, and 1988. Each of the nations had concerns about how the

UNCG would affect its sovereignty. It was only during the presidential administration of Ronald Reagan that the US ratified the UNCG, and even then it was not accomplished without a battle in Congress. In fact, the US Senate only agreed to consent to the ratification of the UNCG if a reservation were added that legislation be passed that "conforms American law to the terms of the treaty" (Roberts 1988, 1).

As early as 1948, US President Harry Truman sent the international treaty of the UNCG to the Senate for approval, but the Senate failed to approve it. And, in fact, every US president from Harry Truman through Ronald Reagan (Harry Truman, John F. Kennedy, Lyndon Johnson, Richard Nixon, Gerald Ford, Jimmy Carter, and Ronald Reagan) was in favor of ratification, with the sole exception of Dwight D. Eisenhower. Be that as it may, from 1949 through 1988, a host of concerns were generated by various Members of Congress about the sagacity of ratifying the UNCG. For example, in 1949, "serious questions [were] raised about the implications of its ratification for the US Constitution" (LeBlanc 1991, 128). More specifically, many Members of Congress were concerned that human rights conventions such as the UNCG might end up abrogating certain key elements of the US Constitution.

Furthermore, in the early 1950s, various Members of Congress asserted that they were discomfited by the definition of genocide as spelled out in the UNCG, while also looking askance at Lemkin himself. For example,

In 1950, one [Senate Committee on Foreign Relations] member, Senator H. Alexander Smith (R., New Jersey), observed that he and others were troubled by the definition of the "new idea" of genocide. Moreover, he could not understand why the "biggest propagandist" for the Genocide Convention should be "a man who comes from a foreign country who ... speaks broken English." Smith claimed that he knew of "many people who have been irritated no end by this fellow running around." Although [Smith] was "sympathetic with the Jewish people," he believed that "they ought not to be the ones who are propagandizing [the Convention], and they are." (LeBlanc 1991, 20)

It was also during Senate hearings in January and February of 1950 that Senator Bourke Hickenlooper (R–IA) and others expressed doubt that "the subject matter of the Genocide Convention was truly a matter of international concern" (Subcommittee of the Senate Committee on Foreign Relations 1971, 106–11).[5]

It is important to recognize that various Members of Congress were not the only ones who either looked askance at the ratification of the UNCG by the United States or were outright opposed to its ratification. A case in point is that, beginning in the early 1950s, the American Bar Association (ABA), a voluntary organization of lawyers, law students, and others, was among the strongest opponents of the ratification of the UNCG in the United States. Various representatives of the ABA had different reasons for opposing the ratification: "concern that provisions of the convention might be used to attack discriminatory legislation [against African Americans] then prevalent in the United States" (LeBlanc 1991, 130); confusion over that which constituted "a part of a group" (41); worry over "the intentions and future prospects of the United Nations in the field of human rights, particularly about the drafting of treaties and conventions in this field, which they saw as threatening to national sovereignty" (41); and, concern that "it would probably not be applicable to genocide against national and other groups behind the Iron Curtain" (41). According to the ABA representatives, the Soviet Union would be able "to evade charges of genocide by claiming that its suppression of, say, any national or ethnical[6] group was not directed at the group as such but rather at political opponents of the regime"; and, since political groups were not a protected group under the UNCG, it would provide the Soviets with impunity to commit genocide (41).

The US Senate finally agreed to the ratification of the UNCG on 19 February 1988. During the previous nineteen years, US Senator William Proxmire (D–WI) took the Senate floor every single day that the Senate was in session in order to advocate for the UNCG's ratification by the United States. In all, he gave more than three thousand speeches, each one of which was original. Proxmire retired from Congress in 1988, shortly after which he saw his dream come true.

The incredible number of hours Lemkin worked each day, the fact that he never took a day off to rest, and that he kept up a furious pace for well over a decade are, in and of themselves, astonishing. It is even more astonishing when one realizes that he was not paid a penny to undertake such work. And, beyond that, Lemkin continued to work incessantly and at a torrid pace despite the fact that he was in extremely poor health, which increasingly sapped his strength. For example, in 1938, he was hospitalized with "double pneumonia" (Fussell 2003, para. 79). And immediately after the UN General Assembly in Paris passed the UNCG, Lemkin entered a Paris hospital, suffering from exhaustion. For the last twenty years of his life, he suffered from high blood pressure. As Lemkin said: "As I am devoting all my time to the Genocide Convention, I have not time to take a paying job, and consequently suffer fierce privation.... Poverty and starvation.

My health deteriorates. Living in hotels and furnished rooms.... Increased number of ratifications.... The labors of Sisyphus. I work in isolation, which protects me" (quoted in Ignatieff 2013, para. 3).

For his unique and unwavering endeavors, Lemkin was nominated for the Nobel Peace Prize by the eminent British statesman Winston Churchill in 1951 and 1952. For whatever reason, the Nobel selection committee never saw fit to award Lemkin this honor.

The rest of the 1950s proved to be extremely difficult for Lemkin. Impoverished and in failing health, he seemed to be a forgotten man. For years on end, Lemkin, sick and alone, resided in penury in a dilapidated hotel in New York City. Throughout that time he pushed and pushed himself in an attempt to convince still more nations to ratify the UNCG. With the help of others, he convinced sixty nations in all to ratify the Convention (Fussell 2003, para. 114).

On 28 August 1959, Lemkin died of a heart attack. It is said that only seven people—a few friends and a few relatives—attended Lemkin's funeral (Sayapin 2009, 1162). Lemkin was buried in Mount Hebron Cemetery in Queens, New York, "with a headstone that reads, 'The Father of the Genocide Convention'" (Elder 2016, para. 10).

Hersch Lauterpacht: A Notable International Lawyer Whose Story and Efforts Are Remarkable as They Relate to Crimes against Humanity

We would be remiss if we failed to draw the reader's attention to another remarkable expert in international law who engaged in pioneering efforts related to crimes against humanity. Hersch Lauterpacht (1897–1960)—a Polish-British lawyer, professor of international law at Cambridge University in England, and judge at the International Court of Justice—is considered by many to have been one of the most influential lawyers of the twentieth century. In relation to the focus of this book, what is most notable about Lauterpacht is that he was instrumental in "enshrining crimes against humanity ... into modern international law" (Sands 2010, 2).

In various ways, Lemkin's and Lauterpacht's biographies sound quite similar. Both were from liberal Jewish families in Eastern Europe; both were born within three years of one another (Lauterpacht in 1897 and Lemkin in 1900); both studied law, though at different points in time, at Jan Kazimierz University; both shared an early interest in international law and published widely on the subject; both men lost a tremendous number of family members in the Holocaust, including their parents; and both contributed, in one way or another, to the Nuremberg War Crimes Tribunals (Troebst

2013, para. 4). Furthermore, both men in their own right are considered to be among "the trail blazers of human rights versus state sovereignty in international law" (Troebst 2013, para. 3, paraphrasing Ana Filipa Vrdoljak 2010, 1165). While Lemkin coined the term "genocide" and prodded the international community to develop and ratify the UNCG, Lauterpacht "most crucially ... crafted the language of Article 6 of the Nuremburg charter, enshrining crimes against humanity, war crimes and the crime of aggression into modern international law" (Sands 2010, 2).

Conclusion

Today, Lemkin is considered a giant figure in the history of humanity. One can say with certainty that if it had not been for Lemkin's vision, selfless dedication, and indefatigable efforts, there would be no UN Convention on the Prevention and Punishment of the Crime of Genocide. That speaks volumes to the power one person can have when he/she/they are willing to pursue his/her/their vision despite all the naysayers and initial setbacks he/she/they may confront.

References

Barbra, Lukunka. 2007. "Ethnocide." *Online Encyclopedia of Mass Violence*, November 3. https://www.sciencespo.fr/mass-violence-war-massacre-resistance/en/document/ethnocide

Barrett, John Q. 2010. "Raphael Lemkin and 'Genocide' at Nuremberg, 1945–1946." In *The Genocide Convention Sixty Years after Its Adoption*, edited by Christoph Safferling and Eckart Conze, 35–54. The Hague: T.M.C. Asser Press.

Cooper, John. 2008. *Raphael Lemkin and the Struggle for the Genocide Convention*. New York: Palgrave Macmillan.

Elder, Tanya. 2016. "Biographical Note." *Guide to the Raphael Lemkin (1900–1959) Collection, 1763-2002 (bulk 1941–1951) P-154.* New York: American Jewish Historical Society. http://findingaids.cjh.org/?pID=109202

Fussell, James. 2003. "Lemkin's War: Origins of the Term 'Genocide.'" March 11. Washington, DC: United States Holocaust Memorial Museum website. https://www.ushmm.org/confront-genocide/speakers-and-events/all-speakers-and-events/lemkins-war-origins-of-the-term-genocide

Ignatieff, Michael. 2013. "The Unsung Hero Who Coined the Term 'Genocide.'" *The New Republic*, September 21, 2013. https://newrepublic.com/article/114424/raphael-lemkin-unsung-hero-who-coined-genocide

LeBlanc, Lawrence J. 1991. *The United States and the Genocide Convention.* Durham, NC: Duke University Press.

Lemkin, Raphael. 1933. "Acts Constituting a General (Transnational) Danger Considered as Offences against the Law of Nations." Translated by Jim

Fussell. http://www.preventgenocide.org/lemkin/madrid1933-english
.htm. Originally published as "Les actes constituant un danger general
(interétatique) consideres comme delites des droit des gens."
—— 1944. *Axis Rule in Occupied Europe: Laws of Occupation—Analysis of
Government—Proposals for Redress*. Washington, DC: Carnegie Endowment
for International Peace, Division of International Law.
—— 2002. "Totally Unofficial Man." In *Pioneers of Genocide Studies*, edited by
Samuel Totten, 365–99. New Brunswick, NJ: Transaction Publishers.
Roberts, Steven V. 1988. "Reagan Signs Bill Ratifying US Genocide Pact." *The
New York Times*, November 5, 1.
Sands, Philippe. 2010. "My Legal Hero: Hersch Lauterpacht." *The Guardian*,
November 10. http://www.guardian.co.uk/law/2010/nov/10
/my-legal-hero-hersch-lauterpacht
Sayapin, Sergey. 2009. "Raphael Lemkin: A Tribute." *European Journal of
International Law* 20 (4): 1157–62.
Schabas, William. 2009. *Genocide in International Law*. 2nd ed. New York:
Cambridge University Press.
Subcommittee of the Senate Committee on Foreign Relations. 1971. Hearing on
the Genocide Convention. 92nd Congress, 1st Session, 106–11. Washington,
DC: Government Printing Office.
Troebst, Stefan. 2013. "Lemkin and Lauterpacht in Lemberg and Later: Pre
- and Post-Holocaust Careers of Two East European International Lawyers."
Tr@nsit, August 26. https://www.iwm.at/transit-online/lemkin-and-lauterpacht
-in-lemberg-and-later-pre-and-post-holocaust-careers-of-two-east-european
-international-lawyers/
United States Holocaust Memorial Museum. 2013. "Sixty-Five Years Later: The UN
Convention on the Prevention and Punishment of Genocide." https://www
.ushmm.org/confront-genocide/genocide-prevention-blog/sixty-five-years-later
Vrdoljak, Ana Filipa. 2010. "Human Rights and Genocide: The Work of
Lauterpacht and Lemkin in Modern International Law." *European Journal of
International Law* 20 (4): 1163–94.
Winter, Jay. 2013. "Raphael Lemkin, a Prophet without Honors." *The Chronicle
of Higher Education*, June 3. https://www.chronicle.com/article/Raphael
-Lemkin-a-Prophet/139515/?cid=cr&utm_medium=en&utm_source=cr

Further Reading on Lemkin, His Life, and His Efforts

Bieńczyk-Missala, Agnieszka, and Dębski, Sławomir, eds (2010). *Rafael Lemkin:
A Hero of Humankind*. Warsaw, Poland: The Polish Institute of International
Affairs.
Ignatieff, Michael. 2000. "The Legacy of Raphael Lemkin." *United States Holocaust
Memorial Museum.*, December 13. https://www.ushmm.org/confront-genocide
/speakers-and-events/all-speakers-and-events/the-legacy-of-raphael-lemkin

Lemkin, Raphael. 2013. *Totally Unofficial: The Autobiography of Raphael Lemkin*. Edited by Donna Lee Frieze. New Haven, CT: Yale University Press.

Schaller, Dominik, and Zimmerer, Jurgen, eds. 2009. *The Origins of Genocide: Raphael Lemkin as a Historian of Mass Violence*. New York: Routledge.

2 | An Overview of the UNCG: An Analysis of Each Article

This chapter examines the components of the United Nations Convention on the Prevention and Punishment of the Crime of Genocide (UNCG; United Nations General Assembly 1948). It presents an interpretive account of the preamble and each article of the UNCG.[7] The analysis of each delineates key implications and/or complications arising from the article. Ultimately, this chapter provides the reader with a basic understanding of the UNCG.

Preamble

The Contracting Parties,
Having considered the declaration made by the General Assembly of the United Nations
in its resolution 96 (I) dated 11 December 1946 that genocide is a crime under
international law, contrary to the spirit and aims of the United Nations and condemned
by the civilized world,
Recognizing that at all periods of history genocide has inflicted great losses on humanity,
and
Being convinced that, in order to liberate mankind from such an odious scourge,
international co-operation is required,
Hereby agree as hereinafter provided.

The preamble links the UNCG to an earlier declaration against genocide made by the UN General Assembly in 1946. The 1946 resolution characterized genocide as an international crime—that is, a crime that, regardless of where it occurs, is of concern to all members of the international community. The preamble further claims that genocide is condemned by the "civilized world." Despite the problem of using the prejudicial term "civilized," this statement does convey the point that genocide goes against what should be considered the basic moral standards of all human societies.

The preamble further declares that genocide has occurred in all periods of history. This is a crucial point for three main reasons. First, it makes clear that genocide is an ongoing problem faced by humanity rather than a rare exception, which supports the case for an active international effort against such a menace. Second, it does not establish a hierarchy among the various cases of genocide, but rather suggests an overarching history of genocide. This is notable in not conforming to a popular presumption that the Holocaust, with its unique features, is the standard against which to evaluate all other cases of mass violence. Rather, it implies that events do not need to be similar to, or mirror images of, the Holocaust in order to qualify as genocide. Third, it makes clear that the drafters of the UNCG and all of the Contracting Parties signing it considered it completely appropriate, as a matter of linguistic accuracy, to apply the term "genocide" to events that occurred prior to the drafting of the UNCG, prior to the event driving its passage (i.e., the Holocaust), prior to the modern era, *and* prior to its entry into force.

There is an important qualification of this last point, however. In its 3 February 2015 Judgment in the *Application of the Convention on the Prevention and Punishment of the Crime of Genocide (Croatia v. Serbia)*, the International Court of Justice (ICJ) indicates that the UNCG cannot be applied retroactively in *legal* cases. Specifically, paragraph 95 of this decision states:

> The Court considers that a treaty obligation that requires a State to prevent something from happening cannot logically apply to events that occurred prior to the date on which that State became bound by that obligation; what has already happened cannot be prevented. Logic, as well as the presumption against retroactivity of treaty obligations enshrined in Article 28 of the Vienna Convention on the Law of Treaties, thus points clearly to the conclusion that the obligation to prevent genocide can be applicable only to acts that might occur after the Convention has entered into force for the State in question. Nothing in the text of the Genocide Convention or the *travaux preparatoires* [the official documents that include the actual wording of the negotiations, drafting process, and discussions during the process of creating the treaty] suggests a different conclusion. Nor does the fact that the Convention was intended to confirm obligations that already existed in customary international law. (International Court of Justice 2015, 50)

While some international law experts have argued that the UNCG can be applied retroactively, this ICJ decision rejects this view and presumably will be followed in legal cases going forward. The wording in the passage above means that no state can be legally bound by the Convention for actions taken before that state became a party to the Convention. Because the UNCG came into force on 12 January 1951, this is the earliest date of any act that a state that was an original party to the UNCG could be held responsible for via the legal system. For states that became parties after the original entry into force of the UNCG, the date the state became a party to the UNCG determines the cutoff for acts to which the UNCG can be applied in legal cases involving that state.

Thus, though the UNCG concept and definition of genocide can be applied to events before 12 January 1951, legal cases applying the UNCG to events prior to 12 January 1951 are not allowable.

Article I

The Contracting Parties confirm that genocide, whether committed in time of peace or in time of war, is a crime under international law which they undertake to prevent and to punish.

This article clearly states that genocide can occur during a period of peace or during a period of military conflict. Historically, war and its aftermath were the typical context of genocide, but in the modern and contemporary eras more and more genocides have been directed inward within a state against one or more minority groups without correlation to an external condition or *formal* declaration of war.

Examples of genocide perpetrated during war are the Armenian genocide, the Holocaust, the 1994 genocide of the Tutsi and moderate Hutu in Rwanda, and the genocide of some eight thousand Muslim boys and men at Srebrenica. Examples of genocide perpetrated during peace include such cases as the genocide of the Aboriginal peoples in Australia, the Soviet human-made famine in Ukraine, and the Indonesian genocide of communists and suspected communists in 1965–66. It is noteworthy that the UNCG's framers made sure to point out that genocide could occur during a period of peace, as the prevailing notion even in the period of the crafting of the UNCG was that mass killing was the function of war or a form of war.

Article I also commits signatories not only to punish the crime of genocide but to prevent it. Ironically, however, prevention is not an emphasis of the UNCG overall, as it is treated in merely one article, VIII, and therein, very briefly.

Article II

In the present Convention, genocide means any of the following acts committed with intent to destroy, in whole or in part, a national, ethnical, racial or religious group,[8] *as such:*

(a) Killing members of the group;

(b) Causing serious bodily or mental harm to members of the group;

(c) Deliberately inflicting on the group conditions of life calculated to bring about its physical destruction in whole or in part;

(d) Imposing measures intended to prevent births within the group;

(e) Forcibly transferring children of the group to another group.

Article II presents the definition of genocide that the UNCG made binding in international law. This definition has been adopted by various tribunals (e.g., the International Criminal Tribunal for the Former Yugoslavia and the International Criminal Tribunal for Rwanda) and courts (e.g., the International Court of Justice and the International Criminal Court) dealing with genocide. Since chapter 3 of this book focuses on the various complexities of Article II and the definition of genocide delineated therein—for instance, what constitutes "intent" and the limiting of the definition of genocide to four types of target group—the following discussion will solely address several general points.

First, genocide attempts to destroy the cohesive existence of a *group*, not merely a set of individuals as individuals. Individuals are targeted because they are members of a group that perpetrators seek to destroy (entirely or partially). While inflicting serious harm against individuals, up to and including murder, deserves universal condemnation, the "*intent to destroy* [a group], *in whole or in part*," is the additional element that sets genocide apart from crimes against humanity, mass murder, massacres, multiple murder, and individual murder. In genocide, then, in addition to the loss of individual lives within the group, the group itself—with its cultural and social structures and contributions—is eliminated from its place in humanity. And that, of course, is to the detriment of all humanity.

A group is destroyed when it is either entirely erased *or* its identity has been changed fundamentally. Thus even when some individuals of a group may survive, genocide still significantly damages (or, in the words of the UNCG, still destroys, at least in part) the group. In some cases, groups may be destroyed to such an extent that survivors are forced to adopt new identities in new groups. The latter has been the experience, for instance, of smaller Indigenous groups. It is important to recognize, however, that according to the UNCG, cultural destruction alone is not genocide. As discussed in chapter 1, while Raphael Lemkin and many subsequent scholars have considered cultural destruction a form of genocide, it was excluded from the UNCG in the drafting process. Put another way, the focus on physical destruction is clear in the wording of Article II.

Second, the killing comprising a genocide does not need to be direct. For example, while many Jews were killed in the Holocaust by being gassed or machine-gunned down, many also died of starvation, disease, overwork, exposure to freezing weather, and so on. The UNCG recognizes that the deaths resulting from the conditions in the Nazi concentration and death camps were every bit as much a part of the genocidal process as those caused by the systematic gassing of inmates. Similarly, when the Turkish authorities began deporting Armenians into vast and barren deserts without adequate water, food, clothing, shelter, or other necessities in 1915, the intent was to kill off the deportees as a result of extreme exhaustion, heat prostration, dehydration, freezing (due to the cold nights), starvation, and/or illness. Again, those dying in these ways were victims of the genocide just as much as those bayoneted, shot, or burned to death.

Third, actions listed as constituting genocide under the UNCG include those means that are not directly lethal in every instance. Paragraphs II(b), (d), and (e) of the UNCG concern such actions. For example, Paragraph II(b), "*causing serious bodily or mental harm to members of the group,*" indicates that psychological torment can and does, under certain conditions, contribute to the process of group destruction. An example of such nonlethal yet profoundly devastating violence—with both a physical and psychological impact—is sexualized violence such as rape and gang rape. In addition to the pain and physical maladies (e.g., the destruction of reproductive organs, infections, and catastrophic illnesses, such as AIDS), such attacks often result in long-term traumatic reactions. The latter can cause a victim to experience severe and long-term depression and/or to withdraw from family and community relations. The fact of the sexual attack itself may result in the stigmatization of the victim within a victim's family and community, thereby eroding social cohesion and identification with the group. This is exactly the case in Darfur, Sudan, where any type of "premarital relations"—including rape—is grounds for both a woman's arrest and exclusion from her family and the larger community.[9]

Pregnancies resulting from rape create additional problems, particularly in regard to the status of the babies born as a result of women being raped. However innocent they are, children born of rape can be reminders of the savagery of the perpetrators, and thus create undue and unfair animosity against the child by the mother and/or larger community. This was the case time and again in relation to the babies born as a result of rape during the 1994 Hutu-perpetrated Rwandan genocide against the Tutsis. Such babies were actually referred to as "rape babies" (Mukamana and Brysiewicz 2008). In Darfur, babies born as a result of rape are often referred to as "Janjaweed babies" (Scheffer 2008, 8) after the name of the militia that carried out attacks against the black Africans of Darfur alongside Government of Sudan troops. All too often the rape victim is either expelled from her home or departs as a result of the animosity directed at her and her child, leaving both the mother and baby bereft while attempting to eke out an existence.

Paragraph II(d), "[i]mposing measures intended to prevent births within the group," is important because it emphasizes that, even if many current members of a group are not killed or dispersed, the group can be destroyed by cutting off its continuation into the future. When perpetrators are cognizant of the fact that the rape of girls and women in certain societies (e.g., fundamentalist Islamic societies) often result in the victims becoming pariahs in their families, local communities, and beyond, and they rape the females with this in mind, it is a clear case of intentionally "imposing measures intended to prevent births within the group." In such cases, perpetrators know that such females will no longer be considered part of the group (married women may be disowned by their husbands, and unmarried girls and women will be deemed "soiled" and thus unmarriageable) and will be prevented from bearing children within the group.

Forced sterilization is another method by which groups can be reduced or eliminated.

Finally, Paragraph II(e), "forcibly transferring children of the group to another group," may also result in destroying in whole or in part the existence of a group without direct killing. This was the case in Australia when thousands of children were taken from their families and communities to be raised within white society in order to strip them of their Aboriginal cultural and ways. It was an effort to make the children more like white people. In this manner, a group's identity as well as the social relations among the original group members are destroyed, with the intent or result of the physical elimination of the original group over time.

In practice, international authorities tend not to recognize a situation as constituting genocide in which there is no direct or indirect killing of at least of some members. That said, an extremely significant counterexample of this was the International Criminal Tribunal for Rwanda's historic judgment in

September 1998 in *Prosecutor v. Jean-Paul Akayesu*. In the judgment, rape was defined as an act of genocide, and the court found the defendant, Akayesu, guilty of genocide on the basis of overseeing and encouraging acts of rape and sexual violence (International Criminal Tribunal for Rwanda 1998, ch. 6.3.1, 496). It should be noted, however, that this judgment was rendered in a context in which there was overwhelming evidence of an overarching genocide that included the direct killing of hundreds of thousands of people; without that kind of context, it is unlikely that rape alone during a conflict would legally be considered a case of genocide. However, that is for a court to decide. If, for example, a court determined that the rapes were intentionally carried out with the intent to destroy the group in whole or in part, a case could very well be made that such criminal acts constituted genocide.

Article III

The following acts shall be punishable:

(a) Genocide;
(b) Conspiracy to commit genocide;
(c) Direct and public incitement to commit genocide;
(d) Attempt to commit genocide;
(e) Complicity in genocide.

Article III follows the standard approach to murder in liberal legal traditions. That is, prosecution is not solely limited to the end result of genocide. When an individual participates in the planning of genocide or otherwise conspires to accomplish the goal of genocide, he/she/they are liable for prosecution. Similarly, the *attempt to commit* genocide is prosecutable. An example of the latter is when a genocide is thwarted by timely intervention that stanches the process of violence early on. The attempt itself, no matter what the result, is prosecutable.

On a different note, "complicity in genocide" refers to any situation in which a person provides support for a genocide without necessarily being a direct perpetrator. For instance, appeals judges of the International Criminal Tribunal for the Former Yugoslavia found Bosnian Serb General Radislav Krstić guilty of "complicity in genocide." While prosecutors in the original trial did not adequately prove that Krstić had genocidal intent in relation to the massacre at Srebrenica in July 1995, the prosecutors did show that Krstić was aware of the genocidal intent of other Drina Corps staff members and did not prevent them from using "Drina Corps personnel and resources to facilitate" the massacre (Voice of America 2009).

Inclusion of such actions in the UNCG is especially important because, unlike murder, genocide is a social form of violence, as odd as it may sound: it requires multiple perpetrators working in concert, along with logistical support. Of special relevance is Paragraph III(c), *"direct and public incitement to commit genocide."* This recognizes that groups—or even entire societies—are not necessarily predisposed toward genocide, and so motivating a population to commit violence against a target group is often essential in order to create a large enough perpetrator base to execute a plan for genocide. Even if those inciting others to commit genocide do not participate in the subsequent acts of genocide, such as killing, international law perceives them to have still contributed crucially to the genocidal process. An important example of this type of incitement is the role Radio Télévision Libre des Mille Collines played in the 1994 genocide in Rwanda vis-à-vis its effort to mobilize the killers. Not only did this radio station broadcast a heavy stream of anti-Tutsi propaganda over the airwaves prior to the genocide, but it continued to do so on a daily basis throughout the genocide. It went as far as calling Hutus to "work," a euphemism for killing. In certain cases, it broadcast the addresses and license plate numbers of certain individuals (usually well-known Tutsis or moderate Hutu who were leaders in the community and perceived as traitors by the radicals) that it wanted killed on a particular day. While liberal democracies usually protect all sorts of speech, including that which promotes prejudicial and even racist viewpoints, governments typically draw the line at concrete incitement to violence. Similarly, Article III includes wording that concerns the prosecution of those helping to carry out genocide through verbal incitement. In such cases, speech that incites individuals to commit genocidal acts is properly recognized as part of the destructive process of genocide.

It is important to recognize that, while Article III is not limited to individuals and Article IX indicates that states can be prosecuted, the articles that stipulate the parameters of prosecution concern individuals, not states. While Article IX implies that a state might be found responsible for genocide, this possibility is merely mentioned, without an explanation of what this would mean that parallels the treatment of this issue for individuals in Articles IV through VII. This is crucial, as prosecution of individuals typically does not address the full responsibility of a state for genocide. Just as genocide targets *groups* of individuals as members of the group, it is perpetrated by *groups* of individuals acting with some measure of coordination. Cases of genocide are rife where that is exactly what took place, including, for example, the following: the Armenian genocide (1915–23), the Soviet manmade famine in Ukraine (1932–33), the Holocaust, the 1994 genocide in Rwanda, the Darfur genocide (2003 to the present day), the Yazidi genocide (2014), and the Rohingya genocide in Myanmar (2016 to the present day).

Article IV

Persons committing genocide or any of the other acts enumerated in Article III shall be punished, whether they are constitutionally responsible rulers, public officials or private individuals.

Article IV emphasizes an important element of the UNCG: *any* individual, regardless of his/her/their position in a society or government, can be prosecuted if he/she/they are alleged to have committed one of the acts listed in Article III. Indeed, the use of the wording "shall" rather than "may" implies that it is the responsibility of the international community to prosecute even heads of state alleged to have committed one of the Article III violations. In 2009, for instance, Omar al-Bashir, then the sitting president of Sudan, was indicted by the International Criminal Court (ICC) on the charge of genocide for his leadership role in the destruction of black Africans in the Darfur region of Sudan from March 2003 to at least 14 July 2008.

The al-Bashir case illustrates one of the problems with the UNCG: its lack of enforcement mechanisms. The same is true of the ICC, which is the main permanent international mechanism for applying the UNCG. In regard to the latter, al-Bashir continued to serve as Sudan's president through early 2019, at which time he was forced from office by internal pressures which had nothing to do with the genocide. Because the ICC does not have the mandate to arrest those it indicts and must rely on states that are signatories to the Rome Statute (the international agreement that created the ICC) to arrest indictees, al-Bashir has remained free, since no state has been willing to arrest and turn him over to the ICC.

It is important to recognize that this is a gap in the UNCG. First it must be said that laws and treaties generally do not include an explicit agreement for enforcement of their provisions. In Canada and the United States, for instance, criminal statutes are written without explicit discussion of the mechanisms to be used, but this is because those mechanisms are understood to already exist (e.g., police forces, court systems, etc.). When the UNCG came into force, there was neither a "world police force" (and there still isn't to this day) or a "world prosecutor" to apprehend and bring to trial alleged violators. Indeed, it wasn't until 1998 that the global community finally created a world criminal court, the ICC, with a specific mandate to try cases of genocide, but even the ICC does not have a police force that can apprehend alleged law violators. (The issue of enforcement will be considered in more detail later in this book.)

Article V

The Contracting Parties undertake to enact, in accordance with their respective Constitutions, the necessary legislation to give effect to the provisions of the present Convention, and, in particular, to provide effective penalties for persons guilty of genocide or any of the other acts enumerated in Article III.

This provision is important for four main reasons. First, those who crafted the UNCG did not create a permanent international court for trying genocide cases, nor did they even specify that an ad hoc tribunal be created when a case was recognized as possibly genocidal in nature. Furthermore, the UNCG does not provide guidance regarding the parameters of such a court or tribunal. Instead, the UNCG cites the judicial systems of Contracting Parties as possible venues for genocide trials.

Second, inclusion of Article V commits each Contracting Party to create the legal mechanisms necessary for prosecuting alleged perpetrators of genocide, including those from its own society. While the text of this article does not extend beyond the requirement for signatories to enact legislation that puts into effect the provisions set out by the UNCG and to spell out "effective penalties" for those found guilty of genocide, it could be interpreted as going farther. For example, Article V could be read as committing each signatory to the UNCG to have judges, prosecutors, and defense attorneys who are conversant with the UNCG and willing to try alleged suspects of genocide, prosecute the latter to the full extent of the law, and incarcerate them if found guilty.

Third, the requirement of effective penalties emphasizes the seriousness of the crime and commits Contracting Parties to respond with a penalty commensurate with the crime of genocide. In other words, a defendant who is found guilty of genocide should not be given a trivial penalty.

Fourth, this article emphasizes the place of state sovereignty in recognizing the jurisdiction of national courts over an international crime, and at the same time requires uniformity across all Contracting Parties in their legal approach to genocide. The most active instance of prosecutions by a national judicial system has been Rwanda's trials of more than one million alleged perpetrators after the 1994 genocide.[10] (This matter is addressed in more detail below, under Article VI.)

Article VI

Persons charged with genocide or any of the other acts enumerated in Article III shall be tried by a competent tribunal of the State in the territory of which the act was committed, or by such international penal tribunals as may have jurisdiction with respect to those Contracting Parties which shall have accepted its jurisdiction.

This article provides three options for trying alleged individual perpetrators of genocide. First, given that Contracting Parties to the UNCG are required to institute national laws largely mirroring the UNCG (Article V), a given country could try perpetrators of a genocide committed on its territory. This has been the case in a number of genocides, including the Bangladesh genocide, the Khmer Rouge–perpetrated genocide in Cambodia, and, in part, the Hutu-perpetrated genocide against the Tutsis and moderate Hutus in Rwanda. As mentioned above, Rwanda tried a vast number of cases of those who allegedly perpetrated genocide in Rwanda in 1994. In fact, two different types of courts within Rwanda handled various cases of alleged *genocidaires*: (1) Rwanda's *national courts*, which tried those accused of planning the geno cide and/or committing serious atrocities, including rape, and (2) the *gacaca* system, which was a community-based process that tried individuals from the local community who allegedly took part in the killing and committed their crimes in the locale where the hearings were held.

Second, Article VI allows for the establishment of a temporary international court to try perpetrators of a specific case of genocide. Two such courts were established in the 1990s in order to try individuals alleged to have committed genocide and crimes against humanity: one to handle cases dealing with the war in the former Yugoslavia, and another to handle cases in relation to the 1994 cataclysm in Rwanda. These were, respectively, the International Criminal Tribunal for the Former Yugoslavia (ICTY) and the International Criminal Tribunal for Rwanda (ICTR). Each of these international criminal tribunals tried both planners of the crimes perpetrated during the events and many of the high-level leaders who carried them out.

Third, Article VI allows for a future permanent international criminal court with jurisdiction over genocide. While there was no such court when the UNCG came into force in 1951, the 1998 Rome Statute established the

ICC. This court has a specific statute, informed by the UNCG, for trying cases of alleged genocide.

The second and third options were seen as crucial in the event that certain governments would be unwilling to try those associated with their countries or in the event that genocide had been "committed by individuals acting as organizers of the State or with the support or toleration of the State" (Kuper 1981, 37). In such cases, relying on domestic courts could result in "the absurd position of the future criminal being entrusted with ensuring his own punishment" (Kuper 1981, 37–38). Historically, trials for state-driven genocides have taken place only after a significant change in the government drove the perpetrators from power and influence.

Article VII

Genocide and the other acts enumerated in Article III shall not be considered as political crimes for the purpose of extradition. The Contracting Parties pledge themselves in such cases to grant extradition in accordance with their laws and treaties in force.

Article VII signifies that any country in which an alleged genocide perpetrator is located will extradite that perpetrator for trial in the country in which the genocide occurred or by an international court. In that regard, this article is supposed to guarantee that no country bound by the UNCG can serve as a safe haven for an alleged perpetrator of genocide who has been accused by a court in any other country bound by the convention or by an international court. This article, in combination with Article V, which requires Contracting Parties to enact legislation that gives force to the UNCG, requires Contracting Parties to remove any legal barriers to extradition of indicted alleged genocide perpetrators. At the same time, it also indicates that extradition can depend on the laws and treaties (presumably including the UNCG) between countries.

An additional point should be made. While Article VII does not provide for "universal jurisdiction" for genocide, that is, allowing any appropriate legal entity to enforce the UNCG anywhere in the world without being prevented by the sovereignty of any given state, Amnesty International (2001) argues that, prior to the UNCG's entry into force, the principle of universal jurisdiction already applied to serious international crimes under what is termed "international customary law"—that is, legal principles that bind even if not codified by formal statute—and thus universal jurisdiction extended to genocide once the UNCG was adopted (7). The International Court of Justice has in essence agreed with this appraisal (Amnesty International 2001, 3).

The Amnesty International report, "Genocide: The Legal Basis for Universal Jurisdiction" (2001), also asserts that the prohibition of genocide is now *jus cogens* (3); that is, it is a fundamental principle of international law that cannot be overridden, ignored, or jettisoned (United Nations 1969, 155). Moreover, a *jus cogens* norm "can be modified only by a subsequent *norm* of general international law having the same character" (United Nations 1969, 155). As noted international legal scholar Cherif Bassiouni (1997) puts it:

> The legal literature discloses that the following international crimes are *jus cogens*: aggression, genocide, crimes against humanity, war crimes, piracy, slavery and slave-related practices, and torture. Sufficient legal basis exists to reach the conclusion that all these crimes are part of *jus cogens*. This legal basis consists of the following: (1) international pronouncements, or what can be called international *opinio juris*, reflecting the recognition that these crimes are deemed part of general customary law; (2) language in preambles or other provisions of treaties applicable to these crimes which indicates these crimes' higher status in international law; (3) the large number of states which have ratified treaties related to these crimes; and, (4) the ad hoc international investigations and prosecutions of perpetrators of these crimes. (68)

Thus, even though the UNCG does not specifically spell out these points, under international law—as it currently stands—no government or area of the world can declare itself or its territory to be exempt from the UNCG, while any court in any country or area can claim jurisdiction over a case of genocide to which the UNCG can be applied.

Article VIII

Any Contracting Party may call upon the competent organs of the United Nations to take such action under the Charter of the United Nations as they consider appropriate for the prevention and suppression of acts of genocide or any of the other acts enumerated in Article III.

This is a particularly important article, as it indicates that signatories to the UNCG have the right to call on the UN to undertake acts of prevention and/òr intervention in the face of potential or actual acts of genocide. This article became of particular importance in 1971 when the Bangladesh genocide was perpetrated by Pakistan, in 1975 and beyond once the international community discovered that the Khmer Rouge had killed their own people in Cambodia, and in the 1990s as both the genocide in Rwanda and the genocide in the former Yugoslavia unfolded. Unfortunately, the debates about intervention on the Security Council and elsewhere did not result in decisive, timely action in any of these cases.

After previous failures and in an effort to make good on the promise of prevention contained in this article, the then UN Secretary-General Kofi Annan created a plan of action in 2004 to prevent genocide (Secretary-General 2004). In this way, the UN leadership took the initiative in crafting genocide prevention policies as a means of encouraging member states to adopt measures and support UN efforts to prevent and suppress genocide.

The five initiatives Secretary-General Annan outlined constitutes the key areas of emphasis of the United Nations in preventing genocide:

♦ Preventing armed conflict,
♦ Protecting civilians during armed conflict,
♦ Ending impunity for those who have committed genocide,
♦ Creating mechanisms to ensure "early and clear warning," and
♦ Taking "swift and decisive action" when genocide is happening or about to happen.

These elements suggest the most obvious approach of deploying UN forces and calling on member states to undertake political or military action to stop an emerging or ongoing genocide. But other, less direct means of prevention are intended as well. For instance, in order to prevent armed conflict, the Secretary-General (2004) calls on the UN and its member states to "attack the roots of violence and genocide: hatred, intolerance, racism, tyranny, and the dehumanizing public discourse that denies whole groups of people their dignity and their rights."

A central component of the Secretary-General's efforts was the 2004 creation of the new position of Special Adviser on the Prevention of Genocide who reports directly to the Secretary-General and the General Assembly. The responsibilities of the Special Adviser are to:

(a) collect existing information, in particular from within the United Nations system, on massive and serious violations of human rights and international humanitarian law of ethnic and racial origin that, if not prevented or halted, might lead to genocide; (b) act as an early warning mechanism to the Secretary-General, and, through the Secretary-General to the Security Council, by bringing to the latter's attention potential situations that could result in genocide; (c) make recommendations to the Security Council, through the Secretary-General, on actions to prevent or halt genocide; (d) liaise with the United Nations system on activities for the prevention of genocide and work to enhance the United Nations capacity to analyze and manage information relating to genocide or related crimes. (Commission on Human Rights of the Economic and Social Council of the United Nations 2006, 4)

The Special Adviser on the Prevention of Genocide shares the Office on Genocide Prevention and the Responsibility to Protect with the Special Adviser on the Responsibility to Protect. In simple terms, the Responsibility to Protect (R2P) principle holds that all governments have a responsibility to ensure the basic rights, security of life, and essential well-being of all within their territories, and, that if they fail to do so, the international community has not just the right but the responsibility to intervene to ensure these things. Clearly, if applied effectively, efficiently, and in a timely manner, R2P could serve as an important tool against genocide.

Despite committed work by each of the Special Advisers on the Prevention of Genocide appointed beginning in 2004, the United Nations and member states still struggle to turn the words of Article VIII into actual life-saving action. The challenges of implementation of Article VIII are discussed in chapter 3 as one of the complexities of the UNCG.

Article IX

Disputes between the Contracting Parties relating to the interpretation, application or fulfilment of the present Convention, including those relating to the responsibility of a State for genocide or for any of the other acts enumerated in Article III, shall be submitted to the International Court of Justice at the request of any of the parties to the dispute.

The UN's International Court of Justice (ICJ) was created solely to handle legal cases between countries. The ICJ may issue advisory opinions or final case decisions regarding issues put to it, depending on the request made to it. It does not address any cases regarding individuals.

Article IX specifies that the ICJ is the body that resolves any formal disagreement between two states regarding the UNCG. This could mean a dispute over whether an actual genocide occurred or not or whether a particular state is responsible for a genocide that did occur. An example of this arose in the 2007 judgment, *Application of the Convention on the Prevention and Punishment of the Crime of Genocide (Bosnia and Herzegovina v. Serbia and Montenegro)*, in which Bosnia filed a case at the ICJ claiming that the new state of Yugoslavia (Serbia) had perpetrated genocide against Bosnians in the 1990s, a charge that Serbia contested.

Article IX works in conjunction with Article VI to ensure that both individual perpetrators and perpetrator states can be held liable for genocide, depending on the circumstances. Article IX is the only place in the UNCG where state responsibility is explicitly mentioned, though the issue is not well-developed therein. At the same time, four full articles (IV through VII) are devoted to a relatively detailed treatment of the issue of individual responsibility. As explained in the commentary on Article III, the focus of the UNCG as a whole is mainly on individual perpetrators.

Article X

The present Convention, of which the Chinese, English, French, Russian and Spanish texts are equally authentic, shall bear the date of 9 December 1948.

The above date, 9 December 1948, should not be confused with the date on which the UNCG came into force after twenty states became signatories to it, which was 12 January 1951.

Article XI

The present Convention shall be open until 31 December 1949 for signature on behalf of any Member of the United Nations and of any non-member State to which an invitation to sign has been addressed by the General Assembly.

The present Convention shall be ratified, and the instruments of ratification shall be deposited with the Secretary-General of the United Nations.

After 1 January 1950, the present Convention may be acceded to on behalf of any Member of the United Nations and of any non-member State which has received an invitation as aforesaid. Instruments of accession shall be deposited with the Secretary-General of the United Nations.

This article indicates that there will be a period during which states can sign the treaty, but even after that period, additional countries, even those that did not exist at the time of the drafting of the UNCG, can become parties to the treaty. It must be emphasized, however, that a state signing or otherwise becoming a party to this or any other international agreement is not the same as that state ratifying it. A representative of a government might sign or accede to a treaty, but the treaty is not officially approved by the government until the said government confirms that it agrees to be bound by what the representative has signed or acceded to. For instance, the United States signed the UNCG on 11 December 1948, but did not ratify it until 5 November 1988.

The provision for nonmember states to ratify the UNCG has become less relevant, as the vast majority of states now in existence are members of the United Nations.

Article XII

Any Contracting Party may at any time, by notification addressed to the Secretary-General of the United Nations, extend the application of the present Convention to all or any of the territories for the conduct of whose foreign relations that Contracting Party is responsible.

Article XII refers to colonized societies—that is, societies controlled by a state without being a part of the state in the sense of its population having the same rights as those in the state. In a striking omission, the UNCG did not automatically apply to the territories still under the control of such countries as Great Britain (Bahamas, Bermuda, Botswana, Belize, Ghana, Kenya, Kuwait, Malaysia, Burma, Tanzania, Zimbabwe, Yemen, Uganda, and Hong Kong, among others), Portugal (East Timor and Mozambique, among others), France (Morocco, Algeria, Tunisia, Laos, Cambodia, and Vietnam, among others), and the United States (Puerto Rico, Hawaii, Alaska, Okinawa, Panama, and the Dominican Republic, among others), despite the fact that the oppression and violence often used to keep various colonies subjugated (and thus, the general world order in place) had, in certain cases, been genocidal in nature. Moreover, the decision of whether or not to extend the UNCG to cover a subject territory was left to the colonizer.

Article XIII

On the day when the first twenty instruments of ratification or accession have been deposited, the Secretary-General shall draw up a process-verbal and transmit a copy thereof to each Member of the United Nations and to each of the non-member States contemplated in Article XI.

The present Convention shall come into force on the ninetieth day following the date of deposit of the twentieth instrument of ratification or accession.

Any ratification or accession effected subsequent to the latter date shall become effective on the ninetieth day following the deposit of the instrument of ratification or accession.

This article is self-explanatory.

Article XIV

The present Convention shall remain in effect for a period of ten years as from the date of its coming into force.

It shall thereafter remain in force for successive periods of five years for such Contracting Parties as have not denounced it at least six months before the expiration of the current period.

Denunciation shall be effected by a written notification addressed to the Secretary-General of the United Nations.

According to Raphael Lemkin (2012), the jurist who coined the term "genocide" and fought to bring about the establishment of the UNCG, Article XIV was included in the UNCG by those opposed to the UNCG (175–76). It opened the door for those who failed to defeat the drafting, signing, and then ratification of the treaty to terminate it in the future. To date, no signatory state has ever denounced the UNCG, and thus it has remained in force.

Article XV

If, as a result of denunciations, the number of Parties to the present Convention should become less than sixteen, the Convention shall cease to be in force as from the date on which the last of these denunciations shall become effective.

While it was the hope of opponents who inserted Articles XIV and XV late in the UNCG drafting process that the articles would be acted upon, Article XV has never been triggered. Furthermore, the large number of states that have ratified or acceded to the UNCG (149) to date makes it highly unlikely that it will be in the future.

Article XVI

A request for the revision of the present Convention may be made at any time by any Contracting Party by means of a notification in writing addressed to the Secretary-General.

The General Assembly shall decide upon the steps, if any, to be taken in respect of such request.

According to Lemkin (2012), this article was also inserted by opponents of the UNCG. While this article delineates the method for modifying the UNCG, no such modification has occurred.

Article XVII

The Secretary-General of the United Nations shall notify all Members of the United Nations and the non-member States contemplated in Article XI of the following:

(a) Signatures, ratifications and accessions received in accordance with Article XI;
(b) Notifications received in accordance with Article XII;
(c) The date upon which the present Convention comes into force in accordance with Article XIII;
(d) Denunciations received in accordance with Article XIV;
(e) The abrogation of the Convention in accordance with Article XV;
(f) Notifications received in accordance with Article XVI.

This article is self-explanatory.

Article XVIII

The original of the present Convention shall be deposited in the archives of the United Nations.
   A certified copy of the Convention shall be transmitted to each Member of the United Nations and to each of the non-member States contemplated in Article XI.

This article is self-explanatory.

Article XIX

The present Convention shall be registered by the Secretary-General of the United Nations on the date of its coming into force.

This article is self-explanatory.

References

Amnesty International. 2001. "Genocide: The Legal Basis for Universal Jurisdiction." In *Universal Jurisdiction: The Duty of States to Enact and Implement Legislation*. AI Index: IOR 53/010/2001. https://www.amnesty.org/en/documents/IOR53/010/2001/en/
Bassiouni, Cherif. 1997. "International Crimes: *Jus Cogens* and *Obligatio Erga Omnes*." *Law and Contemporary Problems* 59 (4): 63–74.
Commission on Human Rights of the Economic and Social Council of the United Nations. 2006. "Promotion and Protection of Human Rights: Report of the

Secretary-General on the Implementation of the Five Point Action Plan and the Activities of the Special Adviser on the Prevention of Genocide." E/CN.4 /2006/84. March 9. https://documents-dds-ny.un.org/doc/UNDOC/GEN /G06/117/05/pdf/G0611705.pdf?OpenElement

International Court of Justice. 2007. *Application of the Convention on the Prevention and Punishment of the Crime of Genocide (Bosnia and Herzegovina v. Serbia and Montenegro)*. Judgment, February 26. *I.C.J. Reports*, p. 43.

International Court of Justice. 2015. *Application of the Convention on the Prevention and Punishment of the Crime of Genocide (Croatia v. Serbia)*. Judgment, 3 February. *I.C.J. Reports*, p. 3.

International Criminal Tribunal for Rwanda. 1998. *Prosecutor v. Akayesu* Case No. ICTR-96-4-T, Judgment (Trial Chamber), September 2, Arusha, Tanzania.

International Peace Conference. 1899. *Convention (II) with Respect to the Laws and Customs of War on Land and Its Annex: Regulations Concerning the Laws and Customs of War on Land*. The Hague. July 29. https://ihl-databases.icrc.org /applic/ihl/ihl.nsf/Treaty.xsp?action=openDocument&documentId= CD0F6C83F96FB459C12563CD002D66A1

International Peace Conference. 1907. *Convention (IV) Respecting the Laws and Customs of War on Land and Its Annex: Regulations Concerning the Laws and Customs of War on Land*. The Hague. October 18. https://ihl-databases.icrc. org/applic/ihl/ihl.nsf/Treaty.xsp?action=openDocument&documentId =4D47F92DF3966A7EC12563CD002D6788

Kuper, Leo. 1981. *Genocide*. New Haven, CT: Yale University Press.

Lemkin, Raphael. 2012. *Totally Unofficial: The Autobiography of Raphael Lemkin*. Edited by Donna-Lee Frieze. New Haven, CT: Yale University Press.

Mukamana, Donatilla, and Petra Brysiewicz. 2008. "The Lived Experience of Genocide Rape Survivors in Rwanda." *Journal of Nursing Scholarship* 40 (4): 379–84.

Schabas, William A. 2009. *Genocide in International Law: The Crime of Crimes*. 2nd ed. New York: Cambridge University Press.

—— 2010. "Retroactive Application of the Genocide Convention." *University of St Thomas Journal of Law and Public Policy* 4 (2): 36–59.

Scheffer, David. 2008. "Rape as Genocide in Darfur." *Los Angeles Times*, November 13, 8.

Secretary-General of the United Nations. 2004. Press release. SG/SM/9197 AFR /893. HR/CN/1077. July 4. https://www.un.org/en/genocideprevention /documents/about-us/Doc.2_Press%20Release_SG%20Plan%20of%20Action.pdf

United Nations. 1969. *1969 Vienna Convention on the Law of Treaties*. UN Doc. A/CN.4/L.682, at 155. New York: United Nations.

United Nations General Assembly. 1948. *Convention on the Prevention and Punishment of the Crime of Genocide*. December 9. United Nations Treaty Series, vol. 78, p. 277 (A/RES/260). New York: United Nations.

United Nations Office on Genocide Prevention and the Responsibility to Protect. n.d. "Responsibility to Protect: About." https://www.un.org/en/genocideprevention /about-responsibility-to-protect.shtml

Voice of America. 2009. "Former Bosnian-Serb General Found Guilty for Complicity in Genocide — 2004-04-19." October 30. https://www.voanews.com/a/a-13-a -2004-04-19-14-1/292398.html

3 The Complexities Inherent in the UNCG

An international convention dealing with an issue as complex and involved as the prevention and punishment of the crime of genocide is, understandably, likely to address issues and concerns about which various actors (national leaders, diplomats, military leaders, and scholars, among others) have vastly different perspectives. That was the case during the crafting and passage of the UNCG (1947–48) as well as during the UNCG's ratification period (1951 to present). It is also, of course, equally true of the implementation of the UNCG vis-à-vis attempts at prevention and punishment.

The crafting and passage of the UNCG proved to be a long process involving ample debate and compromise. Due to the fact that different nations had vastly different and often intractable opinions as to what the genocide convention should and should not address, it is hardly surprising that it went through numerous iterations. Ultimately, as a direct result of the give and take (i.e., deal-making and tradeoffs) during the drafting process, the UNCG came to be perceived as a "compromise" document.

The result of this process was a complex document filled with subtle shadings of meaning as well as compromised components left intentionally vague or ambiguous. If an interpreter of the Convention—be it a student, a scholar, the president of a country, a member of government, a UN official, and so on—does not fully understand the meaning of key words and phrases in the UNCG as well as its more challenging elements, then there is no way that he/she/they can ever hope to make reliable judgments about what does and does not constitute genocide.

This chapter probes the issues that have proved to be the most contentious since the passage of the UNCG in 1948. Most of them, interestingly, concern Article II of the UNCG. Article II spells out the acts that constitute genocide, when such acts are committed with intent to destroy, in whole or in part, a national, ethnic, racial, or religious group as such. Those acts, as described in Article II, are as follows:

(a) *Killing members of the group;*
(b) *Causing serious bodily or mental harm to members of the group;*
(c) *Deliberately inflicting on the group conditions of life calculated to bring about its physical destruction in whole or in part;*
(d) *Imposing measures intended to prevent births within the group;* [and]
(e) *Forcibly transferring children of the group to another group.*

Our purpose in this chapter is twofold: (1) to provide readers with a clear sense of the most complex issues inherent in the UNCG, and (2) to provide readers with the means to accurately apply the wording of the UNCG to potential and actual cases of genocide. In order not to weigh readers down with every minutia germane to the drafting process, we purposely focus on what we perceive as the most important issues, debates, and decisions regarding that process.

The Issue of Intent

In part, Article II of the UNCG reads as follows: "*In the present Convention, genocide means any of the following acts committed* with intent *to destroy, in whole or in part, a national, ethnical, racial or religious group, as such …*" (emphasis added). Without a solid understanding of the issue of intent and its primacy for determining whether a case of mass murder or another action constitutes genocide or not, it is impossible to truly grasp the concept of genocide.

It is important to recognize that "under the Anglo-American legal system, a crime (no matter whether it is armed robbery, manslaughter or genocide) requires both a guilty act (*actus reus*) and a guilty mind (*mens rea*)" (Scott 2013, 6). The latter is commonly referred to as the "criminal intent requirement." In order "to win a conviction, a prosecutor must prove beyond a reasonable doubt that the accused committed a prohibited act with *criminal intent*" (6; emphasis added).

In the eyes of the law, intent is *not* synonymous with motive. Many tend to confuse the two terms, but to thoroughly understand the UNCG one needs to understand the distinction between "intent" and "motive."

Simply put, "intention" is equated with *the express or deliberate* undertaking of an action. Intention, then, constitutes the deliberate plan or objective of the individual carrying out the action—what he/she/they hope the result to be; indeed, what he/she/they plan to happen (e.g., wiping out an entire group of people or forcing a group of people off their land or from a nation). It is a conscious *and* a purposeful act; that is, it is neither unintentional nor accidental. As mentioned above, intent constitutes what lawyers refer to as the *mens reus*, or the mental state of the individual carrying out the action. *Intent is key to ascertaining criminal responsibility.*

"Motive," on the other hand, is what *drives* the intent of the actor in carrying out the crime. Put another way, motive is the underlying reason for carrying out the act. Motive, then, refers to the catalyst or stimulus (i.e., hatred, rage, jealousy, retribution, etc.) for carrying out a particular act. Motive is *not* key to determining criminal responsibility. It should also be noted that different members of the group perpetrating a genocide might have different motives, but share one intent: the destruction, in whole or in part, of the targeted group(s). Motive is *why* an individual or group pursues genocide, while intent is confirmed by the mere fact that he/she/they are pursuing genocide, regardless of the reasons.

Since the distinction between motive and intent is often misconstrued, the following example should prove helpful in differentiating the two. In the case of the Ottoman Turkish genocide of the Armenians (1915–23), there is ample evidence that the central leadership of the Ottoman Turkish perpetrators (formally known as the Committee of Union and Progress or CUP) intended the destruction of the Armenians. Such evidence is clearly spelled out in the orders issued by the CUP.

But as for the perpetrators' motives, there has been legitimate debate among scholars as to what induced the perpetrators to intend the destruction of the Armenians. Good cases can be made that they were motivated by, among other influences, (1) an ultranationalist, exclusivist ideology that required complete Turkification of the Ottoman Empire and the "removal" of the Armenian presence, (2) economic gain, or (3) resentment at the weakened state of the Ottoman Empire and fear of its dissolution. The fact that—at least given the current state of research—it is not possible to determine the exact motive(s) in a definitive manner does not mean that the intent of the perpetrators to commit genocide is not clear and unequivocal.

On a different note, it is important to recognize that intent can be mistaken for premeditation, but these are not the same either. In some instances, genocides appear to evolve from lesser human rights violations.

In this sense, prior to the eruption of genocide, perpetrators may not have envisioned carrying out a genocide. Yet, at some point, perpetrators come to intend genocide by embracing the process and moving it forward. In this way, a genocide would be intended but not premeditated. Premeditated genocides, as was the case in Rwanda in 1994, clearly occur, but when studying these cases, it is still important to keep the issues of premeditation and intent separate.

Regarding intent, criminal law becomes more complex when the question of negligence and acts of omission come into play. For example, debate continues apace as to whether the refusal to prevent a certain harm that is likely to destroy in whole or in part a protected group can be considered the requisite intent. Ethicist James Rachels (1995) has famously argued that deciding to allow someone to die when the person might have been saved is morally equivalent to actively killing the individual. At the same time, case law appears generally to consider "intent" as manifested in action rather than omission.

Second, in criminal law there is what is referred to as (a) "basic (or general) intent" and (b) "specific intent" (which is also referred to as "special intent"). Basic or general intent refers to a case in which the defendant allegedly intended to commit an illegal act. Therefore, basic or general intent *does not focus on* whether or not the defendant intended to cause this or that result due to his/her/their action. Thus, if a perpetrator acts with the intention to commit a criminal act but is void of the desire to obtain a particular result, the individual has acted with general intent. An armed robbery could be an example. A person intends to rob a convenience store with a firearm. This is the general intent. If, in the process of doing so, the person shoots and injures a store clerk, the specific result of injuring the store clerk was not part of the general intent.

On the other hand, specific or special intent (which from this point forward will simply be referred to as "specific intent") is something altogether different. Specific intent typically involves a defendant *intentionally committing an act for the specific purpose of causing a particular result when committing that act*. Specific intent requires not simply intending to commit an act but acting with a particular goal in mind—that is, intentionally committing the act with the intent of achieving a particular goal. Article II of the UNCG is concerned with specific intent. Thus, in relation to the UNCG, specific intent is present when the defendant acts with the intent specifically to destroy a protected group, in whole or in part.[11] In this regard, scholar Alexander K.A. Greenawalt (1999) asserts that genocide "is a crime of specific or special intent, involving a perpetrator who specifically targets victims on the basis of their group identity with a deliberate desire to inflict destruction upon the group itself" (2264).

Put another way, if either of the words "intent" or "destroy" were removed from Article II, then the crime being described *could not* and *would not*, under international law, be considered a case of genocide. Thus, for example, if a perpetrator killed a massive number of people within the same group but had *no intention of destroying the group, in whole or in part*, then the crime could not and would not be deemed, under international law, genocide. As Nehemiah Robinson (1960) asserted in a major commentary on genocide, "acts of destruction would not be classified as Genocide unless the intent to destroy the group existed or could be proven regardless of the results achieved" (58–59). It is not the mass deaths that indicate that a genocide has occurred, but *the intention to destroy a group in whole or in part* that does.

A significant challenge comes when there is evidence that perpetrators were aware of the group status of those they used violence against but never acknowledged such group status as the explicit reason for the violence. For instance, when accused of committing genocide against the Aché people, an Indigenous group in the Amazon, the Paraguayan government responded that the killings and other destruction of Aché were not intended to destroy them, as such, but rather were coincidental to the goal of taking their lands in the name of development (Gilbert 2006, 118; Totten, Parsons, and Hitchcock 2002, 63). In other words, the intent was purportedly not genocide of the group but rather land theft. The perpetrators intended to use genocide to serve a goal beyond the genocide. Scholars often refer to such genocides that serve some further goal as "instrumental"; that is, instruments for the attainment of a distinct goal. That does not make these occurrences any less cases of genocide, because genocide is intentionally chosen as the means to that further goal. In the case of the Aché, in order to get to the ultimate goal of appropriating the Aché's land, the perpetrators chose to commit genocide with the goal of eliminating the Aché's presence on the land.

While the drafters of the UNCG did not spell out what they meant by "intent" in Article II, those who more recently drafted Article 30 of the Rome Statute of the new International Criminal Court did. More specifically, "Article 30 of the Rome Statute declares that the *mens rea* or mental element of genocide has two components, *knowledge* and *intent*. According to Article 30, 'a person has intent where: (a) *In relation to conduct*, that person means to engage in the conduct; and, (b) *In relation to a consequence*, that person means to cause that consequence or is aware that it will occur in the ordinary course of events'" (quoted in Schabas 2009, 242). It is important to note that, in this clarification, if an intentionally chosen set of actions is likely to result in the destruction in whole or part of a group, and those committing those actions are aware of the likelihood of that result, then intent is present. This could be seen to cover what might be termed "negligent genocide" in response to the issue raised above.

A question that often arises is, "How, exactly, does one ascertain or prove 'intent'?" This is a crucial question not only in regard to bringing perpetrators to justice in the aftermath of a genocide but also for efforts to intervene in what could be an ongoing genocide. More often than not, perpetrators *do not* leave behind a written record of their intentions or plans.[12] This has especially been true since the advent of the UNCG, for, as noted earlier, many of those who plan a genocide, order it, and oversee it are shrewd enough to know that leaving behind such a record could lead to their indictment for genocide.

In the event that perpetrators do not leave behind a paper trail or other hard evidence (e.g., statements made at public rallies caught on video or audio), prosecutors and courts must rely on other types of evidence. More specifically, judicial bodies (i.e., the ICC, the ICTR, and the ICTY) carrying out trials of alleged *genocidaires* (see ICTR 1998, 1999, 2001) have made use of various details and factors that reflect intent, including but not limited to the following: "the methodical way of planning"; "the general political doctrine which gave rise to the acts"; "words and deeds"; "a purposeful pattern of actions"; "the repetition of destructive acts"; "the systematic manner of killing"; "the scale of atrocities committed"; "the systematic targeting of victims on account of their membership in a particular group, while not targeting members of other groups"; "the relative proportionate scale of the actual or attempted destruction of a group"; and so on. The idea is that such features of a situation would not have occurred had there not been the underlying intent to destroy a group in whole or in part.

Sometimes such efforts pay off, and sometimes not. That is, sometimes prosecutors present enough significant information based on one or more of the aforementioned categories and put all of the pieces together in a way that convinces the judges of the intent of the perpetrators. In other cases, prosecutors are unable to locate enough pieces of evidence or evidence that is sufficiently convincing and thus are not able to demonstrate intent adequately enough to satisfy the appropriate legal standard.

Perhaps one of the clearest confirmations of the importance of intent in actual court cases was evidenced during the *Prosecutor v. Bagilishema* case at the ICTR. On 7 June 2001, the Chamber of the Court (the panel of judges hearing the case) stated "that a crime of genocide is proven if it is established beyond reasonable doubt that, firstly, one of the acts listed under Article 2(2) of the Statute was committed and, secondly, that this act was committed against a specifically targeted group [protected under the UNCG], with the specific intent to destroy, in whole or in part, that group. Genocide therefore invites analysis under two headings: the prohibited underlying acts and the specific genocidal intent or *dolus specialis*" (International Criminal Tribunal for Rwanda 2001b, para. 55).

The Focus of Genocide and Thus of the UNCG: Groups, Not Individuals

What is absolutely essential to understand is that the UNCG's focus is the destruction of groups (particular groups), *not individuals* per se.

Individuals, of course, are treated horrifically during a genocidal process, and individuals, of course, make up groups. Be that as it may, Raphael Lemkin's express purpose in coining the term "genocide" was to zero in on his ardent concern for the safety of groups. More specifically, when Lemkin (1944) first coined the term "genocide," he defined genocide as "a coordinated plan of different actions aiming at the destruction of essential foundations of the life of national groups, with the aim of annihilating the groups themselves" (80). Thus, harm to individuals is genocidal when the reason for this harm is that the individuals are members of a protected group *and* when the destruction of the group is the aim of the actions taken against individuals.

Even when a group, as such, is destroyed "in part," it opens the door to the demise of the group as a viable entity. In the case of the destruction of part of a group, if a substantial number of members of the group is destroyed, it could make it extremely difficult, if not impossible, for the survivors to continue as a fully functioning group. Concomitantly, if members of a group that have certain significance for the functioning or identity of the group—those members who constitute the leadership of the group, religious leaders, the educated elite, and so on—are eliminated, then, again, it may well prove extremely difficult, if not impossible, to continue as a group. (This issue will be revisited later in this chapter in much more detail.)

In one case after another dealing with genocide at the ICC, the ICTR, and the ICTY, the primacy of the group has been driven home. In the first international conviction for genocide, the ICTR emphasized the primacy of the group by asserting that "the victim of the crime of genocide is the group itself" (International Criminal Tribunal for Rwanda 2001a, para. 521).

It is important to note that the jurisprudence of the ICTR and ICTY used two different methods for determining whether a group could be classified as a national, racial, ethnic, or religious group: the objective and subjective. The objective approach is predicated on the members being born into the group. The subjective approach is predicated on its members perceiving themselves as being members of a particular group (self-identification) and/or being perceived by the perpetrator group as a particular group (identification by outsiders/others). The objective method is what is generally used in courts, but there are times when the subjective is introduced. It is also true that there are times (though infrequent) when a combination of objective and subjective methods is used. The subjective method in regard to how perpetrators define the groups they are targeting is intimately connected to their intent, and thus perhaps should be recognized as an indicator of intent.

A classic example of the subjective method arose in the case of the Darfur genocide (2003–). While the perpetrators—Government of Sudan leaders, military troops, and the Janjaweed (hired militia comprised of mercenaries, among others)—and the victims—the so-called black Africans of Darfur (composed of members of the Fur, Zaghawa, and Massaleit tribal groups)—were all dark-skinned and Muslim, both the perpetrators and the victims perceived themselves as distinct groups. More specifically, the perpetrators considered themselves to be Arab or red, while perceiving those in Darfur as being black. Similarly, the victim group saw the attackers as Arab or red, and themselves as black.

On a final note, it also important to recognize that "as far as the group's right to exist is concerned, the harm has occurred once a perpetrator forms the intent to destroy a group and commits one of the acts enumerated in the Convention. It does not matter at all whether the genocidal intent was part of a plan, perpetrated by a state or by private parties, successful or reasonably likely to succeed, vast in scope or small in the number of victims" (Alonzo-Maizlish 2002, 1380). Thus, once the perpetrator "commits one of the acts enumerated" with the intent to destroy the group, he/she/they are automatically culpable for having attempted to commit genocide and could be tried for having done so.

The Term "Destroy"

A key term in Article II of the UNCG is "destroy": "to destroy, in whole or in part ...." Here it is critical to understand that an attack against a group in one of the four protected categories *does not constitute genocide if the perpetrator had no intention of destroying*, in whole or in part, the group as such. (The four groups, as discussed in note 8, are racial groups, ethnic groups, religious groups, and national groups.) That, of course, does not preclude the fact that a crime or a mass human rights violation has occurred, but rather that the crime committed is something other than genocide.

Simply put, attacking, murdering, massacring, or causing the disappearance of people who are members of a particular group protected by the UNCG does not rise to the level of genocide unless such attacks, murders, massacres, or disappearances are committed against such people *because* they are members of a group covered by the UNCG *and* as a means towards destruction of that group in whole or in part.

As for the concept of "destroy," killing is not the only type of destructive act delineated in the UNCG. Over and above (a) "*killing members of the group*," the other methods of destruction included in Article II of the UNCG are:

(b) Causing serious bodily or mental harm to members of the group;

(c) Deliberately inflicting on the group conditions of life calculated to bring about its physical destruction in whole or in part;

(d) Imposing measures intended to prevent births within the group;

(e) Forcibly transferring children of the group to another group.

Direct Killing Is Not the Only Way to Commit Genocide

As various committees worked on the drafts of the UNCG and different actors provided commentary on these drafts, there was ample debate over which "*acts committed with intent to destroy, in whole or in part*" should constitute genocide. In the years since, many who come to the UNCG for the first time are either taken aback by or baffled by some of the acts listed under Article II.

More often than not, other than scholars and legal experts, most people who discuss genocide seem to think that mass killing is the primary, if not the only, act that constitutes genocide. But that simply is not the case. The nature of genocidal destruction can be, in fact, much more complicated than killing.

Article II(b): Causing serious bodily or mental harm to members of the group.
The first element of the statement ("*causing serious bodily ... harm*") is generally easily understood. It refers to serious physical harm that does not result in death. It can, but does not have to, refer to infliction of permanent physical damage.

Prior to settling on the exact wording "serious harm," a host of other options, more or less in the same realm of physical harm, were considered by the drafters, including, for example, "mutilations and biological experiments imposed for other than curative purposes" (Secretariat draft), "impairing physical integrity" (proposed by Belgium), "the infliction of physical injury or pursuit of biological experiments" (proposed by the Soviet Union), "causing grievous bodily harm to members of the group" (Great Britain), and "causing serious bodily harm to members of the group" (India). Significantly, "the principle that the Convention punish serious acts of physical violence falling short of actual killing was affirmed without difficulty" (Schabas 2009, 181). The drafters appreciated that there is more than one way (i.e., killing) to perpetrate genocide. And from there they attempted to ascertain exactly what actions had been used during the course of genocides in the past.

The meaning of the second element of the aforementioned statement— "*causing serious ... mental harm*"—is much less evident and more challenging for those who are trying to understand or apply the UNCG. Among the many questions that have been raised in regard to the issue of "*causing serious ... mental harm*" are as follows: What constitutes "serious" mental harm? What type of violence is not likely to result in mental harm of one sort or another? How can serious mental harm of a group be assessed without carrying out large-scale psychiatric tests, and is that feasible?

Tellingly, during the drafting process, several nations expressed bafflement about the meaning of "*causing serious ... mental harm.*" As a result, upon considering the possible ratification of the UNCG, some states chose to attach an "understanding" (a statement of explanation so that the rest of the world was aware of how that particular state understood the phrase/ wording) to their position. The United States did exactly that:

> When the United States Senate was considering ratification of the Convention, in 1950, it proposed the following "understanding": "That the United States Government understands and construes the words 'mental harm' appearing in article II of the Convention to mean physical permanent injury to mental facilities" [*sic*]. When ratifying the Convention [in 1988, during the Reagan administration], the United States formulated the following "understanding": "(2) That the term 'mental harm' in article II(b) means permanent impairment of mental faculties through drugs, torture or similar techniques." (Schabas 2009, 184)

It is most unfortunate that the exact meaning of the words "mental harm" agreed upon by the drafters was not, at the least, included as a foot-note in the UNCG. As it currently stands, far too few individuals (be they the leaders of individual states, members of the media, certain academics, or students) seem to take the time to return to the *travaux préparatoires* (the official documents that include the actual wording of the negotiations, drafting process, and discussions during the process of creating a treaty) in order to ascertain exactly what the drafters meant by specific terms.

It also should be noted that there have been dramatic advances in our understanding of human psychology since the drafting of the UNCG in the late 1940s. Partly in reference to the long-term effects of the Holocaust, the concept of trauma as a psychological injury that results from being subjected to and/or witnessing extreme events (e.g., sexualized violence, mass killings, torture, headless bodies, murder, domestic violence such as spousal and/or child abuse, child sexual abuse, etc.) has emerged in connection to individual and group violence. Such developments appear to be influencing the way that "*serious ... mental harm*" in relation to genocide is understood.

An important evolution in the understanding of this type of destruction has been confirmed by recent legal decisions. When there is the intent by perpetrators to destroy in whole or in part a designated group as such through sexualized violence, which results in serious bodily and/or mental harm, then rape rises to the level of genocide. In genocide after genocide—the Bangladesh genocide (1971), the genocide of the Tutsi and moderate Hutu by the Hutu in Rwanda (1994), the Darfur genocide (2003–), the Yazidi genocide (2014), and the genocide of the Rohingya in Myanmar (2016–19), among many others—there is ample evidence that rape was used to inflict serious bodily and mental harm on women and girls as a means of destroying the group in whole or in part. As for the 1994 genocide in Rwanda, the International Criminal Tribunal for Rwanda found that "rape and sexual violence certainly constitute infliction of serious bodily and mental harm on the victims and are even, according to the [Trial] Chamber, one of the worst ways of inflicting harm on the victim" (International Criminal Tribunal for Rwanda 2001a).

The evidence supporting such a view is, unfortunately, all too ample. In many cases, such as Bangladesh (1971), Rwanda (1994), and Darfur (2003–), many rape victims ended up suffering a number of different maladies, including but not limited to the following: grave injury to their reproductive systems; various sexually transmitted diseases, including HIV/AIDS; internal bleeding; incontinence; and post-traumatic stress.

In Darfur, for example, many of the women and girls who attempted to resist being raped were "reportedly beaten, stabbed or killed" (Amnesty International 2004, par.1, section 3.1). Amnesty International also reported that "when giving birth, [women and girls in Darfur] who have been raped are prone to the problem of fistula. A fistula occurs when the wall between the vagina and the bladder or bowel is ruptured and women lose control of the bladder or bowel functions. They become isolated as a result of their incontinence" (par. 2, section 4.2).

Likewise, many of the victims of the aforementioned cases suffered such horrific injuries that later they were not able to have babies. Finally, many rape victims suffer extremely serious psychological trauma, which can last over the course of their entire lives.[13]

Men and boys are also sometimes victims of sexualized violence that likewise causes serious psychological and physical harm. Their numbers are far below those of female victims, but they are victims nonetheless.

Addressing, in part, the issue of causing serious mental harm, the ICTR (2003) concluded the following in the case against one Ferdinand Nahimana, who had been in charge of Radio Television Libre des Mille Collines:

> In finding Ferdinand Nahimana guilty in the Media Trial at the ICTR for genocide perpetrated in Rwanda in 1994, the Court Chamber reported the following: "Between January and July 1994 Nahimana ... exercised authority and control over RTLM [Radio Television Libre des Mille Collines] content, radio reporters, announcers, etc. (Section 6.20, p. 24). From 1990 until December 1994, Nahimana ... conspired [with others] to work out a plan with the intent to exterminate the civilian Tutsi population and eliminate the moderate Hutu. From July 1993 to July 1994 RTLM broadcasts echoed the description of the Tutsis as the enemy and the members of the opposition as their accomplices, regularly using contemptuous expressions such as *inyenzi* [cockroaches] or *inkotanyi* [supporters of the Rwandan Patriotic Front or RPF] and referring to them as enemies or traitors who deserved to die (Section 5.11, p. 17).... RTLM identified locations where the Tutsis had sought refuge and told the *Interahamwe* militiamen to attack those locations. Several of the locations were attacked and the Tutsis there were massacred. In certain cases, RTLM identified certain individuals who were described as accomplices and told the militiamen to find and execute them (Section 6/15, p. 23).... By the acts described ... Nahimana ... is responsible for the killing and causing of serious bodily or mental harm to members of the Tutsi population with the intent to destroy, in whole or in part, that ethnic or racial group as such, and there by committed GENOCIDE. (Under: Count 2 Genocide, third paragraph, p. 26)

Article II(c): Deliberately inflicting on the group conditions of life calculated to bring about its physical destruction in whole or in part.

As one example among many of this approach to genocide, the Government of Sudan (GoS) and its allied militia, the Janjaweed, wreaked havoc on village after village of black Africans in Darfur (2003–). In doing so, they contaminated wells by tossing dead donkeys into them, plundered and destroyed crops, damaged irrigation systems, and stole or killed cattle, all of which were essential to the survival of the black Africans in Darfur. At the same time, the GoS and the Janjaweed purposely prevented humanitarian aid (i.e., food, medical care, etc.) from reaching the black Africans (Winters 2004, 1). Through these acts, the GoS, with the goal of eliminating the group in whole or part, created conditions that made it much more difficult and often impossible for black Africans in Darfur to survive.

Article II(d): Imposing measures intended to prevent births within the group.
As the Center on Law and Globalization (2007) notes, "Rwandan survivors told stories of sexual mutilation and violent rape that left survivors sterile and physically unable to engage in intercourse. The [ICTR] found that 'sexual mutilation, the practice of sterilization, forced birth control, separation of the sexes, and prohibition of marriages' could be construed as measures to prevent births within the target ethnic group" (n.p.). Such actions destroy the ability of the group to continue to exist into the future as well as undercutting social cohesion among group members in the present by preventing family and broader community development.

Further, the Center on Law and Globalization (2007) notes, the ICTR "also found that in patriarchal societies, where membership of a group is determined by the identity of the father, forced pregnancy through rape can constitute genocide when the intent is for the victim to 'give birth to a child who will consequently not belong to its mother's group'" (n.p.).

On a different note, the culture of some groups includes the perception by both families and the larger community that women and girls who have been raped are pariahs. This is despite the fact that the victims suffered horrific violations and had absolutely no choice in what happened to them. This is true of the Muslim rape victims in Darfur, just as it was true of the Muslim rape victims in the Bangladesh genocide. In the case of Darfur, many, if not most, female rape victims were cast out of their homes and communities because they were perceived as "dirty" or "shameful."

There is also ample evidence that Muslim men in cases such as Bangladesh and Darfur refused to marry such victims, let alone have children with them. In many if not most cases, the perpetrators knew exactly what they were doing and how they were not only causing major tensions within families and communities but also preventing the female victims from having children with men of their faith.

In the Darfur genocide, perpetrators knew that rape victims would end up pariahs in the view of their families and communities and be cast out. Tellingly, the perpetrators actually mocked their female victims by telling them they were raping them so that they would have "tomatoes," or red babies. Even though the attackers were dark-skinned, they perceived themselves as Arabs and thus red, as opposed to black like the so-called black Africans of Darfur.

Babies born as a result of their mother's rape by Government of Sudan troops or the Janjaweed were frequently referred to as "Janjaweed babies." These babies were also pariahs and not welcome in the villages that their mothers came from. Exclusion of these babies from the victims' communities also functioned as a way to prevent births within the victims' communities, though in a different way from cases where women and girls who were raped and suffered physical harm were prevented from becoming pregnant or suffered stigmatization that resulted in their not being marriageable within their own communities and thus unable to have children who were considered black African.

As Kelly Askin (2006) has duly noted, "Rape as an instrument of genocide most often invokes paragraph (b) [of the UNCG] intending to 'destroy a protected group,' and (d) 'imposing measures intended to prevent births within a group'" (150).

On a different but related issue, the chamber hearing the Akayesu case noted that the measures may be mental as well as physical. "For instance, rape can be a measure intended to prevent births when the person [who was] raped refuses subsequently to procreate, in the same way that members of a group can be led, through threats or trauma, not to procreate" (International Criminal Tribunal for Rwanda 2001a, paras. 507–08). While the ICTR statement is problematic in suggesting that a survivor of rape is exercising fully free choice, the broader recognition that various psychological and physical effects of rape can prevent childbearing is an important point.

Article II(e): Forcibly transferring children from one group to another.
One of the most notorious cases of kidnappings during genocide was committed by the Ottoman Turks and their Kurdish militia during the Armenian genocide. Countless Armenian children were taken from their parents and given or sold to Turkish families. Others were orphaned by the killings of their parents and then taken into Turkish homes or orphanages with the aim of making them into Turks. Children old enough to understand themselves as Christians were forced or coerced into denouncing their religion and accepting the Islamic faith. As part of the destruction of their identities,

girls were often forced into lives of domestic servitude and faced sexual abuse in homes and "harems," sexual slavery, and "slave marriages."

Many of the Armenian children were given to Muslim families living in towns and villages from which Armenians had been virtually erased, thus making it easier to "Islamize" the children and prevent them from associating with or seeking help from their fellow Armenians. Some Turkish families acquired Armenian girls as brides for their sons, essentially "Turkifying" them. Also of note is the fact that "Jemal Pasha, a leader of the Young Turks, 'established an orphanage' for the express purpose of Turkifying young Armenian children. Especially for this purpose Jemal invited the Panturkist woman writer Halide Edib, who was well known for her efforts to Islamize and Turkify Armenian orphans, to serve as its directress" (1).

A similar situation took place in Argentina between 1976 and 1983 when Argentina was rocked by what is commonly referred to as the "Dirty War." It was a period when the right-wing military *junta* carried out what were certainly crimes against humanity, and possibly genocide.[14] During that period, up to thirty thousand individuals were openly murdered or "disappeared." The latter were referred to as "*los desaparecidos*" (the disappeared), since the government refused to admit that they had been arrested, tortured, killed, and disposed of in secret locations. The targets were individuals that the regime considered to be leftists, insurgents, and a danger to the welfare of the nation. Most were political activists, intellectuals/academics, members of labor unions, and students who opposed the regime. People were often pulled from their homes or off the street, incarcerated in torture centers, and then tortured and killed. It is estimated that between 1,500 and 2,000 people were drugged and flown out over the Atlantic Ocean, where they were dumped.

Some of those who were kidnapped were women with young children as well as women who were pregnant. Reportedly, pregnant women were allowed to live until they had their babies, and then they were killed. The babies (around five hundred) were often given or sold to military families and to certain others who were deemed "politically acceptable." Before the babies were distributed, false birth certificates were created for them. Some torturers adopted the babies, but in other cases adoptive parents had no idea where their babies came from or the circumstances in which they were born and then orphaned (see Wills 2018).

To date, well over one hundred such children have been identified. Since most of their parents were killed during the Dirty War, many of these individuals have located and reunited with their grandparents. On the other hand, some have refused to leave their adoptive parents, the only parents they have ever known. Those who have not been identified continue to have no idea that they were kidnapped or that their mothers were likely killed by the regime.

While there has been great debate as to whether the crimes committed during the Dirty War constituted genocide or crimes against humanity, what did transpire was horrific and those responsible for overseeing and carrying out the crimes needed to be held accountable. While most individuals who were charged with various violations and whose cases were heard in a court of law were found guilty of crimes against humanity and/or torture, one individual was found guilty of genocide. That was former Argentine Army General Luciano Benjamin Menendez, who, on 28 August 2008, in a federal court before Argentina's northern province of Tucuman, was sentenced to life imprisonment for crimes against humanity, torture, and genocide during the 1976 military rule.

As horrific as the Armenian and Argentine cases, among others, have been, perhaps the most important case relative to Article II(e) is that of the forcible transfer of Aboriginal and Torres Strait Islander children from their families to either government facilities or white families by the Australian government from about 1890 through much of the twentieth century. In 1997, based on this history, the Australian government inquiry into the forcible transfer of children found that its own actions constituted genocide under the UNCG. While there was direct killing of Indigenous peoples in Australia as part of the overarching history of colonization there, various aspects of which are viewed as genocide by many experts, the Australian finding of genocide did not depend on the transfers being part of a broader destruction of Indigenous peoples but was itself the central element considered in the declaration of genocide. Ultimately, "the Inquiry ... concluded that [destruction of the target group] was a primary objective of forcible removals and is the reason they amount to genocide" (Commonwealth of Australia 1997, Chapter 10, para. 15). The report asserted that children are "core elements of the present and future of the community. The removal of these children creates a sense of death and loss in the community, and the community dies too.... There's a sense of hopelessness that becomes part of the experience for that family, that community" (para. 15). Thus, it was the forced removals themselves that constituted genocide under the UNCG.

This long-term removal process was instituted via a number of laws. Its aim was to both assimilate the children into mainstream white

Australian culture (though at its lower levels) and dilute the percentage of Indigenous descent through multigenerational miscegenation toward "biological absorption" by white Australia (Commonwealth of Australia 1997, Chapter 7, paras. 1–3). As statistics regarding the life conditions in the residual communities and the psychological trauma disclosed by those who were removed from their homes (and their family members who remained behind) clearly demonstrate, the effects of this history of removal was devastating for the targeted peoples. In the decades since the report of the government inquiry (Commonwealth of Australia 1997) was published, and despite backlashes by government officials and some in the broader society, sustained efforts by Australia to attempt to address, at least to the extent possible, the effects of this destructive policy have been prominent in the society.

Similar large-scale removals of children through the residential and boarding school systems, respectively, were also perpetrated in Canada and the United States. In recognition of the seriousness of this recent history, in the 2010s Canada instituted a country-wide truth and reconciliation process to address its actions.

The Wording "In Whole or In Part"

Over the years, incredible confusion has surrounded the wording "in whole or in part" in the definition of genocide in the UNCG. It is most unfortunate that the drafters were not more conscientious in spelling out exactly what they meant by "in part," for a great deal of time and energy has been expended by prosecutors, defense lawyers, and judges, not to mention scholars, in discussing and debating the issue while trying to come to some sort of consensus as to what the phrase means.

Many political leaders, journalists, and members of the broader public are under the misconception that genocide refers to the total annihilation of a group of people. It does not. While perpetrators may intend to kill an entire group of people, they are rarely, if ever, successful in doing so. That is, while a genocide could, hypothetically, result in the physical destruction or forced assimilation of every single member of a targeted group, this is rarely, if ever, the case.[15]

First, and foremost, it must be understood that "the term 'in whole or in part' refers to the intent of the perpetrator, *not to the result*" (Schabas 2009, 277; emphasis added). This is similar to what was discussed above in regard to the term "destroy." That is, "it is not necessary to achieve the final result of the destruction of a group in order for a crime of genocide to have been committed. It is enough to have committed any of the acts listed in the article with the clear intention of bringing about the total or partial destruction of a protected group as such" (from the International Law Commission's 1996 report on the draft of Code of Crimes; also quoted in Schabas 2009, 277).

Perhaps this issue is more easily understood when one considers the fact that in one of the most clear-cut cases of genocide in the twentieth century—the Holocaust—the perpetrators (the German Nazis and their collaborators throughout Europe) were not even close to being successful in killing every single Jew in Europe, though this was certainly their aim. While the Nazis and their collaborators carried out the horrific slaughter of close to 6 million Jews during the Holocaust, millions of Jews fortunately survived. Statistically, "according to the *American Jewish Yearbook*, the Jewish population of Europe was about 9.5 million in 1933. In 1950, the Jewish population of Europe was about 3.5 million" (United States Holocaust Memorial Museum n.d., para. 2). Thus while large numbers and/or percentages of the members of targeted groups are often killed during genocides, generally the perpetrators end up killing only a part of the targeted victim group. That, of course, in no way diminishes the significance, let alone the horror, of the number of deaths the perpetrators carried out.

Another example of a genocide that resulted in the killing of a large number of members of a group, but not its entirety, was the case of Guatemala's genocidal actions against the Maya in the early 1980s. Jose Efrain Rios Montt, who served as the president of Guatemala for six months during 1982 and 1983, was tried for genocide and crimes against humanity in a national trial held in Guatemala City in 2013. Rios Montt was charged with genocide in regard to fifteen massacres against the Ixil population in the Quiche region. The charges include "being the intellectual author of the death of 1,771 people, [and] enforced displacement of 29,000" (Amnesty International n.d., para. 7). In May 2012, Rios Montt was indicted with a second charge of genocide for the December 1982 murders of 201 people in Dos Erres. A United Nations–sponsored truth commission conducted in 1999 found that the Government of Guatemala was responsible for acts of genocide in four designated regions in the period between 1981 and 1983. The commission stated that the Guatemalan army identified Mayas as an "internal enemy" and as a base of guerrilla support, and thus committed massacres of members of an ethnic group with the objective of killing the greatest number of people possible in that ethnic group as state policy.

In the Ixil region, between 70 and 90 per cent of the Maya communities were wiped out during this period.[16] At the same time, not every Maya in Guatemala was intended to be killed.

The point, then, of the wording "in whole or in part," is to ensure that, even when a perpetrator group does not intend to destroy every member of a group but rather a critical mass or large subgroup (say, intellectuals, the group's leaders, all men of military age, etc.), this still constitutes genocide because it fundamentally alters and weakens the targeted group as a whole and because those targeted for direct killing are targeted because of their group membership. As Schabas (2001) puts it, "in whole or in part" does not refer to "*the physical act*" of actually destroying all or some members of the group, "as if there must be some quantitative threshold where mass murder turns into genocide, but rather, [to] the intent of the perpetrators" (40; emphasis added). For instance, when men and boys were murdered at Srebrenica in the former Yugoslavia in 1995, they were murdered because they were Bosnian Muslims, and because the Serbs—as part of an overarching expulsion program—wanted to render that group (i.e. the larger group) defenseless and permanently degraded as a group.

Some perpetrators actually discuss what fraction of a group will be targeted directly for genocide. In this regard—particularly during court trials—the words of the perpetrators come back to haunt them. For example, in the trial of Radovan Karadžić, the Appeals Chamber presented evidence regarding the actual words spoken by Karadžić and other alleged members of the joint criminal enterprise that suggested they possessed genocidal intent in their planned elimination of Bosnian Muslims. The Appeals Chamber asserted that the Trial Chamber had received evidence that in meetings at which Karadžić had been present, "*it had been decided that one third of Muslims would be killed, one third would be converted to the Orthodox religion and a third will leave* [the region] *on their own*" (ICTY 2013, para. 8; emphasis in original).

Despite extensive discussion and debate over what exactly the words "in part" mean in the UNCG, no precise standard has been agreed upon. Among the many questions posed over the years, vis-à-vis this issue, are "Legitimately, what is the smallest number that constitutes 'in part'?" and "Is there a certain percentage of people that must be killed in order to move from mass killing or massacre to genocide?" This raises a further question that students studying genocide frequently ask: "If an individual or group has the intent to destroy a particular group, in whole or in part, but only ends up killing three or four people, does that really constitute genocide?" There has been ample debate around this issue by scholars, and most concur that the deaths of three or four would not constitute genocide. Craig Etcheson (1995), a scholar of genocide who served as the Chief of Investigations in the Office of Co-prosecutors at the Extraordinary Chambers in the Courts of Cambodia, which was charged with trying high-level perpetrators of the Khmer Rouge–perpetrated genocide of their fellow Cambodians, sums up the issue as follows:

> There are some ambiguous phrases in the legal definition of genocide, and one of them is particularly troubling: "in whole or in part." One person is a "part." Does that mean that if a criminal intended to kill all the members of a protected group, but succeeding in killing only one single member of that group, that this single killing could constitute genocide? Most legal scholars seem to think that this extreme case would not qualify as genocide. But where does one draw the line? How many members of a group must be killed before those acts rise above the threshold of the definition of genocide? There is no clear answer to that question. (1)

So, where does this leave scholars, judicial personnel, and readers? Many noted scholars over the years have argued that "a part" must be comprised of a "substantive part." Thus, unless a targeted group solely consisted of, for example, roughly thirty to forty members, the killing of three to four people out of hundreds or thousands, while devastating for the individuals, their family members, and others, can hardly be deemed "substantive."

In 1999, the ICTY took this issue on directly and asserted that genocide must involve the intent to destroy a "substantial" part, though it need not constitute a "very important part" (n.p.). That still leaves us shaking our heads without a clear standard. While a very important part is likely to mean, for example, the leaders of the group, religious figures, the most educated (the educated were specifically targeted early on during the Cambodian genocide, for example), or the strongest individuals or those most likely to fight back (in the case of the Armenian genocide, men were the first group to be exterminated by the Ottoman Turks), we are still left with guessing what the phrase "substantial part" means.

One possible—and perhaps the most plausible—interpretation would be to hold that the size and/or role of the part of the group targeted for destruction would have to be integral to the whole group in such a way that its destruction would significantly alter the group identity and its functioning, thus making the group less viable in the long term. (We will return to this point shortly.)

During the Krstić trial at the ICTY (2001), the court asserted that "although the perpetrators of genocide need not seek to destroy the entire group protected by the Convention, they must view the part of the group they wish to destroy as *a distinct entity* which must be eliminated as such" (quoted in Alonzo-Maizlish 2002, 1389; emphasis added). Speaking of this situation, Alonzo-Maizlish (2002) made the following observations:

> The court examined the political events surrounding the massacres in question [at Srebrenica in July 1995], the foreseeable effects of the killings in light of the forced transfers of the surviving members of the community, the cultur-ally specific implications of having the target population removed from the group, the targeting of homes and religious buildings for destruction, and the concealment of mass graves, "thereby preventing any decent burial in accord with religious and ethnic customs and causing terrible distress to the mourning survivors." With such materials before it, the Krstić court concluded that the defendant's forces "sought to eliminate all the Bosnian Muslims in [the geographic location] as a community" even though "only the men of military age were systematically massacred." (1389)

Taking a more pragmatic approach to the issue of "in part," Schabas (2001), who is quoted above as asserting that there isn't "some quantitative threshold where mass murder turns into genocide," goes on to note that "the actual result, in terms of quantity [is] relevant in that it assists the trier [i.e., the court] of fact to draw conclusions about intent based on the behavior of the offender. The greater the number of actual victims, the more plausible becomes the deduction that the perpetrators intended to destroy the group in whole or in part" (40).

International law experts have also argued that the protected group may be perceived in qualitative as well as quantitative terms. In other words, an "important" or a "significant" part of the group could be tar-geted and thus legitimately be considered "in part." During deliberations by the Commission of Experts Established Pursuant to Security Council Resolution 780: Investigating Violations of International Humanitarian Law in the Former Yugoslavia, Professor Cherif Bassiouni (1994), a Commission member, asserted that the Commission considered the defini-tion in the UNCG to be "sufficiently pliable to encompass not only the targeting of an entire group, as stated in the Convention, but also the target-ing of certain segments of a given group, such as the Muslim elite [i.e., lead-ers, the most educated, etc.] or Muslim women" (323–24). This qualitative approach was used in the Jelisić case at the ICTY. The court asserted that the wording "in part" "could be satisfied if the accused targeted 'the most representative members of the target community,' which would include 'the total leadership of a group,' consisting of 'political and administrative leaders, religious leaders, academics and intellectuals, business leaders and others ... regardless of the actual numbers killed'" (quoted in Commission of Experts 1994, para. 94).

As is typical with many issues in international law, scholars and the various personnel (prosecutors, defense attorneys, and judges) involved in court cases related to genocide continue to debate and wrangle over exactly how "in part" should be defined/understood.

Groups That Are and Are Not Protected under the UNCG

One might think that any and all groups of people—no matter how small or large in number, how wide or narrow in conception—would be considered protected groups under the UNCG. That, however, is not the case.

Purportedly, the reasons why the four groups—racial, ethnic, religious, and national—were finally settled on were (1) because each of the groups had, historically, been targeted repeatedly, and (2) because of their ostensible "stability."

In the end, the drafters of the UNCG chose to extend protection solely to those groups that they perceived as "stable" (or, put another way, "permanent") as opposed to those that were perceived as lacking stability or permanence. The fact, though, is that while the drafters considered a wide range of possibilities in regard to which groups to include and not include, their discussions and debates were far from exhaustive. It shouldn't be a surprise that controversy has arisen in regard to why certain types of groups were extended protection while others were not.

A stable or permanent group, it was argued, was one into which one was born. A classic example, they argued, is that individuals are born Caucasian, black, Asian, or Australasian, and even if they wished to do so, they cannot change their race from black to Caucasian or Caucasian to Asian.

An unstable or impermanent group is one that individuals, if they so wished, could move into or out of at any time. For example, US citizens who have declared themselves Republicans at the age of eighteen but later decide to become Democrats in their thirties can easily change their political group and even change again later in life if desired.

Numerous scholars have commented on the fact that the makeup of the four types of groups listed in the UNCG are not only "ambiguous" (Verhoeven 1991, 5) but have also resisted "a precise definition" (Schabas 2009, 124). As Verhoeven (1991) argued, the ambiguity of the terms "is hardly a surprise because the concepts of race, ethnic and national group are *a priori* imprecise" (5). It is no wonder that many of the nations that ended up ratifying the UNCG "defined the groups in different ways" (LeBlanc 1991, 60).

Many examples underscore Verhoeven's (1991) point. The following commentary discusses the various concerns of different delegations working on the UNCG in the late 1940s in regard to the wording of the groups:

> The reference to ethnic groups ... was inserted in Article II at the request of the Swedish delegation during debate in the Sixth Committee. It is not clear from the record precisely why ethnic groups were thought to be so important in their own right, but the Swedish delegation seems to have been concerned about possible future problems in interpreting the word "national" and wanted to draw a distinction between national and ethnic groups. Other representatives, however, argued that the word "ethnic" meant essentially the same thing as the word "racial," and that it was therefore unnecessary to specifically mention ethnic groups because the word "racial" was already in Article II. The drafts of the Convention glossed over these difficulties, however, and adopted the Swedish amendment by a very narrow vote (eighteen in favor, seventeen against, and eleven abstentions). (quoted in Verhoeven 1991, 5)

While the drafters of the UNCG ultimately came to a consensus that membership in a religious group is stable and permanent, in reality that is hardly the case. Depending on the religion and the context, it is very often possible to disaffiliate from a religion as desired, and people do so all of the time. Indeed, it is not uncommon today to meet people who have, for example, left the Catholic Church and converted to Judaism or Buddhism or vice versa. Perhaps the authors of the UNCG thought that in most instances the religion in which people are raised largely dictates what they will remain throughout their lives.

As for national groups, Lawrence J. LeBlanc (1991), a professor of political science at Marquette University, observed that "there seems never to have been any doubt throughout the drafting stage that [national groups] should be identified as an object of protection in Article II. In fact, the matter was never really discussed; it was apparently assumed by everyone concerned that national groups should be covered" (59). Despite the fact that individuals can relinquish or renounce his/her/their nationality and seek to become a citizen of another nation, national groups as a whole are considered both stable and permanent. (Among some of the more famous individuals who have given up their US citizenship are, for example: Moshe Arens, a politician who gave up his US citizenship in order to become the Israeli Ambassador to the United States; Josephine Baker, a singer who renounced her US citizenship because of rampant racism and became a citizen of France; Garry Davis, who famously renounced his US citizenship in order to become "a citizen of the world"; T.S. Eliot, a renowned poet who gave up his US citizenship to become a British citizen; John Huston, an acclaimed film director who renounced his US citizenship to become an Irish citizen; Henry James, a famous novelist who renounced his US citizenship in order to become a British citizen; Yehudi Menuhin, a world-famous violinist who renounced his US citizenship to become a British citizen; and Tina Turner, a rock and roll star who relinquished her US citizenship to become a Swiss citizen).

Second, it is also true that under certain conditions naturalized citizens can have their citizenship revoked. For example, while natural-born citizens in the US cannot have their citizenship revoked, naturalized citizens can. Generally, US citizenship is revoked for one of the following reasons: being a spy, and thus a traitor; allegedly having planned, overseen, and/or committed horrific atrocities during, for example, a case of crimes against humanity or genocide; and/or making false statements on a US visa application. Some of the more notable individuals who were naturalized US citizens and had their US citizenship stripped from them include: John Demjanjuk, who covered up the fact that he was a Nazi concentration camp guard at Sobibor, Majdanek, Flossenburg, and Trawniki, and was thus found guilty of having committed naturalization fraud; Emma Goldman, who was discovered to be an anarchist; Jorge Sousa, who helped carry out the Dos Erres massacre in Guatemala in 1982, and was subsequently found guilty of naturalization fraud by the US government; and Beatrice Munyenyezi, who was found guilty of making false statements to US officials in an attempt to cover up the fact that she selected female Tutsis to be raped and murdered during the 1994 genocide in Rwanda.

During the drafting phase of the UNCG, economic, political, social, and linguistic groups were all put forward as potential groups to be protected under the UNCG, but, after ample discussion, all were rejected. Different representatives during the drafting process had suggested and supported the inclusion of such groups for various reasons. The suggestion of political groups engendered the most prolonged and vociferous debate.

While the first draft of the UNCG did not include the category of political groups, eventually "it was added by a sub-committee of the Sixth Committee" (Schabas 2009, 153). Why it was eventually added is not known. As Schabas has noted, "no reported debate explains this development" (153). But substantial, heated, and prolonged debate occurred once it was included.

While the United States and France were in favor of the inclusion of political groups, a host of other nations either raised objections or simply opposed inclusion, including but not limited to Venezuela, Lebanon, China, the Soviet Union, and Poland.

Three different substantive arguments were made *against* extending protection to political groups under the UNCG:

1. The Soviet Union argued that genocide "solely referred to the destruction of races and nations," and that the inclusion of political groups "would have had the effect of expanding the meaning of the term beyond 'the fundamental notion of genocide recognized by science'" (LeBlanc 1991, 61).
2. Various countries (Egypt, Iran, Venezuela, and Uruguay, among others) argued that political groups lacked both stability and permanence. LeBlanc (1991) writes, "They argued that political groups were different in kind from national, ethnic, racial and religious groups, since persons tend to be born into the latter groups, or at least the membership of these groups does not change over relatively longer periods of time" (62). Countries often, though, had unique takes within the general argument. For example, while China argued that political groups "had neither the stability nor the homogeneity of an ethnical group" (quoted in Schabas 2009, 155), Poland argued that national, racial, and religious groups "had a fully established historical background, but political groups had no such stable form" (quoted in Schabas 2009, 155).
3. Numerous representatives claimed that at some point in the future their governments might need to confront subversives and if they did then they might end up "being called before an international tribunal to answer charges made against them" (LeBlanc 1991, 63).

Other concerns and objections were raised as well, including those by countries that warned that some governments might not agree to ratify the UNCG if it included political groups as a protected group and that inclusion might result in a prolonged debate that would slow down the acceptance and passage of the UNCG.

Ultimately, according to LeBlanc (1991), members of the Sixth Committee argued that "the protection of political groups ought to be considered in the broader context of human rights rather than the narrower one of genocide" (62). LeBlanc goes on to say that "this argument seems to have been introduced as an afterthought—a convenient way of avoiding an issue full of conceptual and political difficulties" (62).

It is also significant that the ambiguities inherent in the four categories reflect a deeper problem. As scholarly research over the past few decades has made clear, there is *no stable definition* of what any of these terms actually means. For instance, Europeans colonizing North America often did not recognize Native American religious practices as legitimate religions at all: "since many tribes had no apparent name for their divinity," it appeared to Europeans that they did not have one (Smith 2004, 118–19). It took US laws in the 1970s and after to recognize Native American religions as true religions deserving of protection under the US Constitution (127). Thus, what qualifies as a "religion" is inherently contested.

Similarly, in the 1980s and 1990s, there was tremendous scholarly debate over what a "nation" actually is, with renowned figures such as Eric Hobsbawm (1992), Benedict Anderson (1991), and Ernest Gellner (1993), as well as many others, offering radically different perspectives, including the view that nations are groups in which members share identity characteristics in conjunction with a shared political outlook (Gellner); the view that nations are "imagined communities," meaning that the fact that members view themselves as part of a given nation actually makes the nation exist (Anderson); and the view that nations are in fact not real social groups but delusions among populations manipulated by elites (Hobsbawm). Debates over the nature of race (see, for example, Mills 1999, 41–66) have included a similar range of notions, while ethnicity has remained less theorized. This is not because ethnicity's meaning is more certain but because it has been seen as even less so and thus as less useful as a political or academic concept.

In the years since the passage of the UNCG by the UN General Assembly in 1948, many scholars have raised critical questions and concerns about a host of issues in relation to the types of groups that are and are not protected under the UNCG. Among the many issues that have been broached and debated are the following: the drafter's understanding or definitions of the protected groups; the lack of precision as to how protected groups are defined and understood; whether all four of the protected groups are truly permanent and stable; and the logic and sagacity (or lack thereof) in issuing protective status solely to the aforementioned four groups (racial, ethnic, religious, and national) while excluding other groups from such protection.

Beginning as early as the 1980s, scholars of genocide urged the international community to consider a revision of the UNCG in order to overcome its restrictive nature. Among the suggestions have been the addition of various types of groups, including political groups, gender groups, professional classes, and economic classes. Thus far, all efforts have come to naught.

The Wording "as Such"

As simple as the words "as such" are, their inclusion in the UNCG has been a point of confusion for many. It is easy to skip right over the words without recognizing their importance.

In the context of the UNCG, "as such" refers to "a separate and distinct entity" (ICTY 1999, para. 79). The words "as such" emphasize and underscore that genocide *requires the intent to destroy a collection of people who have a particular group identity*" (ICTY 2006, para. 20; emphasis added). In other words, it is not the intended destruction of simply any multitude of people but rather of people who form a particular type of group. The "as such" here also reinforces the point that it is because of their particular group membership that a set of people are targeted—they are targeted "as such," that is, as members of a group.

An ICTR case explained the issue a bit differently but came to the same conclusion: the Chamber interpreted "'as such' to mean that the act must be committed against an individual because the individual was a member of a specific group and specifically because he belonged to this group, so that the victim is the group itself, not merely the individual" (ICTR 2003, para. 410).

The UNCG and Prevention

Despite the UNCG title's apparent emphasis on prevention of genocide, in the text of the UNCG prevention has a very small presence, as pointed out in chapter 2. The UNCG's actual de-emphasis on prevention has been reflected in the history of genocide since ratification of the UNCG. To date, the mention of prevention constitutes more lip service than reality. Following the end of World War II and in the aftermath of the Holocaust, a popular and heartfelt admonition that was repeatedly cried out was "Never Again!" After such a shattering crime as the Holocaust, one would think that the world would have worked tirelessly to prevent another genocide. In theory, that's what the world was saying when the UNCG resolution was presented to and passed by the UN General Assembly in 1948. But over the course of the next fifty years, one genocide after another was perpetrated—in Africa, Asia, Central America, North and South America, and Europe.

But then, in 1994, the Rwandan genocide seemed to shake humanity to its core, yet again. In its aftermath, the international community seemed to be emboldened to move beyond simply talking about prevention and punishment and established the ICTR and the ICTY. While they were primarily established to hold alleged *genocidaires* responsible for the crimes they committed, many also hoped that future *genocidaires* would recognize that the tribunals put many planners behind bars, and that they might think twice about carrying out such a heinous crime themselves. Unfortunately, once again, it did not work that way. How so? All four of the following groups suffered genocide following the 1994 genocide in Rwanda: eight thousand Muslim men and boys in Srebrenica (1995), between three and four hundred thousand black Africans of Darfur in Sudan (2003–present), the Yazidis in Iraq (2014), and the Rohingya in Myanmar (2016–present). Many have claimed that the establishment of the ICTY and ICTR was more an attempt by the international community to make up for its sorely inadequate responses to the killings as they occurred in the former Yugoslavia and Rwanda, respectively, than anything else.

Why the failure at prevention? Despite the pretentions of the UNCG, the very structure of the United Nations has limited much in the way of prevention. Within the UN Security Council, the five permanent members (the United States, Great Britain, France, Russia, and China) each have veto power over any resolution that is presented to the Security Council. A single veto by any one of the permanent members (commonly referred to as the P5) defeats the resolution, and there is no route allowed for passing a vetoed resolution.

The mere threat of a veto has thwarted intervention in a host of places, but perhaps most prominently in the case of the 1994 genocide in Rwanda. Even the threat by one of the P5 to cast a veto (some have referred to this as a "hidden veto") can prevent the rest of the members of the UN Security Council from voting against the wishes and aims of that P5 member:

Hidden vetoes can have terrible consequences. The Security Council failed to act during the Rwandan genocide in 1994 due to the hidden vetoes of France and the US. Paris and Washington not only blocked UN action, but also used their hidden veto to weaken the definition of the crisis under international law. An independent UN report admitted that the failure of the Security Council to act led directly to the genocide.... Only after the worst months of the killing did the Security Council endorse *Opération Turquoise*, a deployment of French troops as a "humanitarian" mission under the UN flag. Yet, 800,000 people died because permanent members considered an earlier UN intervention contrary to their interests. A Human Rights Watch report scathingly said: "The Americans were interested in saving money, the Belgians were interested in saving face, and the French were interested in saving their ally, the genocidal government." (Nahory 2004, 1)

It is also important to note that there is a clear distinction between a peacekeeping force, which does not have the mandate to halt atrocities, and a peace enforcement mission, which does have the mandate to attempt to halt atrocities, be they crimes against humanity or genocide. Far too often the UN Security Council votes in favor of a peacekeeping mission versus a peace enforcement mission, and the mission often ends up being a half measure or worse in attempting to quell a potential case of crimes against humanity or genocide.

Conclusion

As readers (including students and professors) delve ever deeper into the issue of genocide, they are bound to continue to come across complex issues that demand close scrutiny of the wording and terms used in the UNCG and interpretations of it. As they become more familiar with the topic of genocide, they, too, are likely to begin to raise critical issues that they want answers to. This will draw them back to the text of the UNCG in order to weigh, wrestle with, and debate the wording in it and what it is supposed to mean. The goal of this chapter was to provide a sound foundation for further exploration as well as to present examples of how such analysis and debate might proceed. For readers who wish to develop their knowledge further, we encourage study of additional work by scholars of international law and/or genocide, as well as case law from the ICTY, ICTR, and ICC.

References

Alonzo-Maizlish, David. 2002. "In Whole or In Part: Group Rights, the Intent Element of Genocide, and the 'Quantitative Criterion.'" *New York University Law Review* 77: 1369–1403.
Amnesty International. 2004. *Sudan, Darfur: Rape as a Weapon of War: Sexual Violence and Its Consequences*. New York: Amnesty International.
— n.d. "Guatemala's Trial of the Decade in Ten Facts." https://www.amnestyusa .org/guatemalas-trial-of-the-decade-in-ten-facts/
Anderson, Benedict. 1991. *Imagined Communities: Reflections on the Origin and Spread of Nationalism*. London: Verso.

Askin, Kelly Dawn. 2006. "Prosecuting Gender Crimes Committed in Darfur: Holding Leaders Accountable for Sexual Violence." In *Genocide in Darfur: Investigating Atrocities in Sudan*, edited by Samuel Totten and Eric Markusen, 141–62. New York: Routledge.

Bassiouni, Cherif M. 1994. "The Commission of Experts Established Pursuant to Security Council Resolution 780: Investigating Violations of International Humanitarian Law in the Former Yugoslavia." *Criminal Law Forum* 279: 323–24.

Center on Law and Globalization. 2007. "Rape May Be an Act of Genocide in International Law." Champaign: University of Illinois College of Law.

Commission of Experts. 1994. *Final Report of the Commission of Experts Established Pursuant to Security Council Resolution 780 (1992)*, U.N. SCOR, U.N. Doc. S/1994/674.

Commonwealth of Australia. 1997. *Bringing Them Home: National Inquiry into the Separation of Aboriginal and Torres Strait Islander Children from Their Families*. https://www.humanrights.gov.au/sites/default/files/content/pdf/social_justice/bringing_them_home_report.pdf

Etcheson, Craig. 1995. "Genocide: By the Law, Not by Emotion." *The Phnom Penh Post*, August 11, p. 1.

Gellner, Ernest. 1993. *Nations and Nationalism*. Ithaca, NY: Cornell University Press.

Gilbert, Jérémie. 2006. *Indigenous Peoples' Land Rights under International Law: From Victims to Actors*. Ardsley, NY: Transnational Publishers.

Greenawalt, Alexander K.A. 1999. "Rethinking Genocidal Intent: The Case for a Knowledge-Based Interpretation." *Columbia Law Review* 99 (8): 2259–94.

Hobsbawm, E.J. 1992. *Nations and Nationalism since 1780: Programme, Myth, Reality*. 2nd ed. Cambridge: Cambridge University Press/Canto.

International Criminal Tribunal for the Former Yugoslavia. 1999. *Prosecutor v. Jelisić*. Case No. IT-95-10-T, Judgment, 19 October. The Hague.

— 2001. *Prosecutor v. Radislav Krstić*. Case No. IT-98-33-T, Judgment (Trial Chamber), 2 August. The Hague.

— 2013. "Appeals Chamber Reverses Radovan Karadžić's Acquittal for Genocide in Municipalities of Bosnia and Herzegovina." Appeals Chamber Press Release (CS/PR1574e), 11 July. The Hague.

International Criminal Tribunal for Rwanda. 1998. *Prosecutor v. Jean-Paul Akayesu*. Case No. ICTR-96-4-T, Judgment (Trial Chamber), September 2. Arusha, Tanzania.

— 1999. *Prosecutor v. Clément Kayishema and Obed Ruzindana*. Case No. ICTR-95-1, Judgment (Trial Chamber II), 21 May. Arusha, Tanzania.

— 2001a. *Prosecutor v. Jean-Paul Akayesu*. Case No. ICTR-96-4-T, Judgment, 1 June. Arusha, Tanzania.

— 2001b. *Prosecutor v. Bagilishema*. Case No. ICTR-95-1A-T, Judgment (Trial Chamber), 7 June. Arusha, Tanzania.

— 2003. *Prosecutor v. Nahimana et al.* Case No. ICTR-99-52, Judgment and Sentence (Trial Chamber), 3 December. Arusha, Tanzania.

— 2005. *Prosecutor v. Mikaeli Muhimana*. Case No. ICTR-95-1B-T, Judgment and Sentence (Trial Chamber), 25 April. Arusha, Tanzania.

International Law Commission. 1996. *Draft Code of Crimes against the Peace and Security of Mankind, Report of the International Law Commission on the Work of Its Forty-Eighth Session*, May 6–July 26, U.N. GAOR, 51st sess., U.N. Doc. A/51/10, art. 17 Commentary 10.

LeBlanc, Lawrence J. 1991. *The United States and the Genocide Convention.* Durham, NC: Duke University Press.

Lemkin, Raphael. 1944. *Axis Rule in Occupied Europe: Laws of Occupation— Analysis of Government—Proposals for Redress.* Washington, DC: Carnegie Endowment for International Peace.

Mills, Charles W. 1999. *The Racial Contract.* Ithaca, NY: Cornell University Press.

Nahory, Celine. 2004. "The Hidden Veto." *Global Policy Forum*, May 1–5. https://www.globalpolicy.org/security-council/42656-the-hidden-veto.html.

Rachels, James. 1995. "Active and Passive Euthanasia." In *Ethical Theory and Social Issues: Historical Texts and Contemporary Readings*, edited by David Theo Goldberg, 471–76. 2nd ed. Orlando, FL: Harcourt Brace.

Reuters. 2016. "Genocide Trial for Guatemala Ex-dictator Rios Montt Suspended." January 11. https://www.reuters.com/article/us-guatemala-trial/genocide-trial -for-guatemala-ex-dictator-rios-montt-suspended-idUSKCN0UP21F20160111

Robinson, Nehemiah. 1960. *The Genocide Convention: A Commentary.* New York: Institute of Jewish Affairs.

Schabas, William. 2001. "Was Genocide Committed in Bosnia and Herzegovina? First Judgment of the International Criminal Tribunal for the Former Yugoslavia." *Fordham International Law Journal* 25 (1): 23–53.

— 2009. *Genocide in International Law: The Crime of Crimes.* 2nd ed. New York: Cambridge University Press.

Smith, Maureen E. 2004. "Crippling the Spirit, Wounding the Soul: Native American Spiritual and Religious Suppression." In *American Indian Thought*, edited by Anne Waters, 116–29. Malden, MA: Blackwell.

Totten, Samuel, William S. Parsons, and Robert K. Hitchcock. 2002. "Confronting Genocide and Ethnocide of Indigenous Peoples: An Interdisciplinary Approach to Definition, Intervention, Prevention, and Advocacy." In *Annihilating Difference: The Anthropology of Genocide*, edited by Alexander Laban Hinton, 54–92. Berkeley: University of California Press.

United States Holocaust Memorial Museum. n.d. "Jewish Population of Europe in 1945." *Holocaust Encyclopedia.* Accessed May 14, 2009. https://www.ushmm .org/wlc/en/article.php?ModuleId=10005687

Verhoeven, Joe. 1991. "Le crime de genocide, originalité et ambiguité." *Revue Belge de Droit International*, 5–26.

Wills, Matthew. 2018. "The Stolen Children of Argentina." *JSTOR Daily*, August 22. https://daily.jstor.org/stolen-children-of-argentina/

Winters, Rogers. 2004. *Testimony before the Committee on Foreign Relations Committee, Subcommittee on Africa, United States Senate.* June 15. http://www.usaid.gov /press/speeches/2004/ty040615-l.html (URL no longer valid.)

4

"Genocide" Distinguished from Other Forms of Major Human Rights Violations: Crimes against Humanity, War Crimes, and Ethnic Cleansing

Based on what has been presented thus far in this book, it should be clear that the term "genocide" has a very specific meaning in the United Nations Convention on the Prevention and Punishment of the Crime of Genocide (UNCG). The definition of "genocide" delineated in the UNCG is the one that is accepted by the international community and legal experts and used in criminal tribunals and courts (both the International Criminal Court and national courts that try *genocidaires*). As a rule, it is also the definition that is used by scholars (e.g., scholars of genocide studies and international law scholars, among others) in their work.

Having a definition that most people accept and make use of in their work is important for a variety of reasons. First, prosecutors and others concerned about punishing the crime of genocide need to have a precise definition so that they can determine whether they believe a person or state has committed genocide. Second, for prosecution of any crime to be recognized as legitimate, a law must include a clear statement of the acts it involves. Third, political leaders, diplomats, human rights organization personnel, and early warning systems operators, among others, need to be conversant with the specifics of the UNCG in order to ascertain whether violence or human rights violations are potentially moving towards genocide. The third reason is particularly significant in that such knowledge can support the issuance of genocide early warnings, activate efforts to staunch a potential or actual genocide, and prompt the immediate rescue of potential victims. Finally, even though some scholars are critical of the UNCG definition of genocide, they generally recognize that it is the necessary starting point for any discussion of alternative definitions. Various scholars have developed alternative definitions explicitly in order to address what they view as flaws in the UNCG definition.

Previous chapters have already considered the ways in which some internal features of the definition of genocide, such as the centrality of the term "intent," affect how the UNCG is understood and applied (or not applied). In this chapter, we direct our attention outward rather than inward to consider key distinctions between genocide and other forms of mass violence and human rights violations.

Terms Existing Prior to the Coining of "Genocide"

There are two categories of related terms: those terms that existed prior to Lemkin's coining the word "genocide," and various legal concepts that are central to human rights law. First, there are the words or phrases that were used prior to the coining of the term "genocide" by Raphael Lemkin and the introduction of it in 1944 upon the publication of his book, *Axis Rule in Occupied Europe*, to describe major cases involving mass killing. These include such terms as "race extermination," "race murder," "extirpation," "pogroms," "slaughter," and "massacres." Even "crime against humanity and civilization"—which, as we will see, evolved into the legal term for a more general category of mass human rights violations: "crimes against humanity"—was used in an official governmental declaration by the United Kingdom, France, and Russia in 1915 in reference to the Ottoman Turkish perpetration of the Armenian genocide.[17]

While we can look back, for example, at Henry Morgenthau's use of "race extermination" to refer to the Armenian genocide he was witnessing (Morgenthau [1915] 2004, 55) and recognize that, as he was using it, the term referred to a set of events that fit the UNCG definition of "genocide," "race extermination" and other such terms are not truly equivalent to "genocide" as we understand it today, for they generally capture only an aspect of genocide, not the entirety of the phenomenon.

For instance, the concept "race extermination" limits genocide to "race"—although Morgenthau ([1915] 2004) appears to use the term in an imprecise sense that includes "nationality" and "ethnic group." Similarly, the emphasis on murder suggests a purely physical destruction that does not convey the destruction of social relations and institutions, culture, and identity that are understood as part of the more encompassing "destruction" emphasized by Lemkin and the UNCG. Under the UNCG definition, genocide not only involves mass killing of members of a group but also attacks the familial, social, political, economic, and religious relations, structures, and institutions binding its members into a group, and thus the group as a group itself.

Along the same lines, even when "pogrom" and "massacre" are used in the plural to indicate a set of these violent events, the true nature of genocide as a systematic series of pogroms or massacres aimed at the overarching destruction of the target group as a group—and not simply the killing of members without reference to a goal or as episodic cases of violence bereft of intention—is not conveyed by such terms.[18]

It is worth noting that, prior to Lemkin's coining of the term "genocide," what we now know—and commonly refer to—as the Armenian genocide was often referred to as "the Armenian massacres." Today, though, that archaic descriptor (i.e., "the Armenian massacres") has specifically been used by some deniers to misrepresent the Armenian genocide as a series of massacres that were neither organized by the central government nor intended to destroy Armenians as a group.

In this regard, then, it is crucial to understand that the inadequacy of such terms as "massacre" and "pogrom," once used to describe a genocidal process, does not in any way mean that genocide was not occurring prior to Lemkin's coining of the term. While deniers purposely twist this fact, so-called "historical relativists"—that is, scholars who mistakenly believe that only terms used in a given era can be applied to events in that era, and thus no event prior to 1944 should be called a "genocide"—confuse the issue. What scholars and students need to understand and appreciate is that the whole point of Lemkin coining the term genocide was to develop a term to use for the many genocides that had occurred prior to 1944 and indeed from ancient times forward (see Theriault 2010, 16–17, 35–36). Lemkin's quest for a term and definition was based on his recognition that previous terms used to describe events that were actually genocides were inadequate as labels.

"Genocide" and Other Related Legal Terms

The second set of terms are legal concepts that are central to human rights law, including "crimes against humanity," "war crimes," and "crimes against peace." Because these have legally precise meanings and because there is a general consensus regarding their meaning in international law, these terms can be compared and contrasted with "genocide."

During the Nuremberg trials, one of three violations that Nazi defendants could be charged with was "crimes against humanity." (The other two were "war crimes" and "crimes against peace.") As noted in chapter 1, Hersch Lauterpacht, an expert on international law, was instrumental in ensuring that "crimes against humanity" was included as one form of crime that the defendants could be charged with. Sands (2010) writes, "Most crucially, [Lauterpacht] crafted the language of Article 6 of the Nuremburg charter, enshrining crimes against humanity, war crimes and the crime of aggression into modern international law" (2).

Crimes against Humanity and Genocide

At the time, "crimes against humanity" consisted of "murder, extermination, enslavement, deportation, and other inhumane acts committed against any civilian population, before or during the war; or persecution on political, racial, or religious grounds in execution of or in connection with any crime within the jurisdiction of the Tribunal, whether or not in violation of domestic law of the country where perpetrated" (International Military Tribunal 1945, Article 6(c)). According to Tomuschat (2006), "Nuremberg opened up a new page of universal history, less than one month after the coming into force of the Charter of the United Nations. By Resolution 95(I) of 11 December 1946, the General Assembly affirmed unanimously 'the principles of international law recognized by the Charter of the Nuremberg Tribunal and the judgment of the Tribunal,' but failed to specify which principles had indeed been so recognized" (836). In 1950, however, the International Law Commission (which had been created under UN Resolution 174) was charged with the task of formulating "the principles of international law recognized in the Charter of the Nuremberg Tribunal and in the judgment of the Tribunal" (UN General Assembly 1947, 112). The final product was formally named "Principles of International Law Recognized in the Charter of the Nürnberg Tribunal and in the Judgment of the Tribunal." It was adopted by the International Commission of Law of the United Nations in 1950 and submitted to the UN General Assembly in the same year.

Just under fifty years later, the international community established the International Criminal Tribunal for the Former Yugoslavia in 1993 and then the International Criminal Tribunal for Rwanda in 1994, both of which included the following crimes within their purview: crimes against humanity, war crimes, and genocide. In 1998, the Rome Statute was approved and established the International Criminal Court, and in 2002, the ICC entered into force. The ICC was mandated with trying crimes against humanity, war crimes, and genocide.

Today, the generally agreed upon definition of "crimes against human-ity" by legal personnel and international law experts is found in the Rome Statute, which states:

> For the purpose of this Statute, "crime against humanity" means any of the following acts when committed as part of a widespread or systematic attack directed against any civilian population, with knowledge of the attack:
>
> (a) Murder;
> (b) Extermination;
> (c) Enslavement;
> (d) Deportation or forcible transfer of population;
> (e) Imprisonment or other severe deprivation of physical liberty in violation of fundamental rules of international law;
> (f) Torture;
> (g) Rape, sexual slavery, enforced prostitution, forced pregnancy, enforced sterilization, or any other form of sexual violence of comparable gravity;
> (h) Persecution against any identifiable group or collectivity on politi-cal, racial, national, ethnic, cultural, religious, gender, as defined in paragraph 3 [not included here], or other grounds that are universally recognized as impermissible under international law, in connection with any act referred to in this paragraph or any crime within the jurisdiction of the Court;
> (i) Enforced disappearance of persons;
> (j) The crime of apartheid;
> (k) Other inhumane acts of a similar character intentionally causing great suffering, or serious injury to body or to mental or physical health. (UN General Assembly 1998, Article 7)

Clearly there is significant overlap between these actions and the acts listed in the UNCG. So how does the definition of "crimes against humanity" differ from that of "genocide"? First, planning and/or carrying out the murder of tens of thousands of people *as individuals* within a civilian population—not as members of a racial, ethnic, national, or religious group but as individuals— would constitute crimes against humanity but not genocide, because genocide is specifically aimed at the targeting of a particular group with the intent to destroy it, in whole or in part, as such.

Second, determining that a crime against humanity has occurred or that a specific individual is guilty of committing a crime against humanity *does not require proof of intent* to destroy in part or in whole a particular group of peo-ple, as such. So, for example, if tens of thousands of people in the same locale are killed by government forces but there is no evidence that the perpetrators had the intent to destroy a particular group in whole or in part, as such, this event would qualify as a crime against humanity but not genocide.

Third, crimes against humanity cover more types of groups than genocide, which is restricted to racial, ethnic, religious, and national groups *only*; mass violence against a political, cultural, gender, or other recognized group is, more often than not, perceived as a crime against humanity, but not genocide, even when the intent to destroy that other type of group is present.

Fourth, establishing that extermination of a group is a "crime against humanity requires proof that the crime was committed as part of a widespread or systematic attack against *a* civilian population; [such] proof is not required in the case of genocide" (*Prosecutor v. Musema*, as quoted in Schabas 2009, 13; emphasis in original). This is the one way in which genocide is seen to have a wider application than crimes against humanity: it does not require that the targets be only civilians. While this last point suggests that some genocides are not crimes against humanity, the key implication is that, in practice, the restriction of genocide to "*the intent to destroy a group, in whole or part*" means that proving genocide in a court of law is much more challenging than proving that a crime against humanity has occurred.

War Crimes and Genocide
A "war crime," according to the Statute of the International Tribunal for the Former Yugoslavia and Rwanda, is a "serious violation of the laws and customs applicable in international armed conflict" and a "serious violation of the laws and customs applicable in an armed conflict not of an international character" (International Committee of the Red Cross, n.d., para. 1). War crimes include such actions as the following:

- the killing of civilians
- the mistreatment or murder of prisoners of war
- sexual assault
- the use of banned biological or chemical weapons
- subjecting persons to humiliating treatment
- maiming persons
- forcing people to undertake work that directly helps the military operations of the enemy
- violation of the right to a fair trial, and
- recruiting children under fifteen years of age into armed forces.

As one can readily ascertain, the concept of "war crime" covers many different acts of varying types. The Rome Statute lists forty-eight distinct actions as "war crimes." The core of the definition is spelled out in the "Geneva Conventions of 12 August 1949," which defines war crimes as:

> any of the following acts against persons (most notably civilians and prisoners of war) or property protected under the provisions of the relevant Geneva Convention:
>
> (i) Willful killing;
> (ii) Torture or inhuman treatment, including biological experiments;
> (iii) Willfully causing great suffering, or serious injury to body or health;
> (iv) Extensive destruction and appropriation of property, not justified by military necessity and carried out unlawfully and wantonly;
> (v) Compelling a prisoner of war or other protected person to serve in the forces of a hostile Power;
> (vi) Willfully depriving a prisoner of war or other protected person of the rights of a fair and regular trial;
> (vii) Unlawful deportation or transfer or unlawful confinement; and
> (viii) Taking of hostages. (UN General Assembly 1998, Article 8)

This list is supplemented by an extensive list of "other serious violations of the laws and customs applicable in international armed conflict, within the established framework of international law" (UN General Assembly 1998, Article 8). These include the protection of active military personnel, by prohibiting:

♦ Killing or wounding treacherously individuals belonging to the hostile nation or army;

♦ Declaring that no quarter will be given;

♦ Employing poison or poisoned weapons;

♦ Employing asphyxiating, poisonous or other gases, and all analogous liquids, materials or devices;

♦ Employing bullets which expand or flatten easily in the human body, such as bullets with a hard envelope which does not entirely cover the core or is pierced with incisions; [and]

♦ Employing weapons, projectiles and material and methods of warfare which are of a nature to cause superfluous injury or unnecessary suffering or which are inherently indiscriminate in violation of the international law of armed conflict (UN General Assembly 1998, Article 8).

The concept of war crimes preexisted the UNCG; in fact, war crimes were addressed and first included in such international agreements as the 1899 and 1907 Hague Conventions.[19]

Just as is true for crimes against humanity, a war crime need not have the same intent to destroy a group, as such, which is requisite for genocide. While many crimes that fall under the definition of "war crimes" could be actions perpetrated during the course of genocide, without the overarching intent to destroy a group, as such, war crimes do not constitute genocide.

Genocides are perpetrated within countries in both times of peace and times of war, while the laws against war crimes, as the term denotes, only apply to acts perpetrated during war, including internal armed conflicts. For instance, the 1965–66 genocide of communists and suspected communists in Indonesia and the 1932–33 Soviet government–imposed famine in the Ukraine were *not* linked to wars.

Crimes against Peace and Genocide

That genocide can take place during peacetime does not mean that genocide is properly categorized as what is called a "crime against peace." Crimes against peace are specifically germane to war: a crime against peace is an unjustified initiation of war against another country. The Nuremberg Military Tribunal defined "crimes against peace" as

> the initiation of invasions of other countries and wars of aggression in violation of international laws and treaties, including but not limited to planning, preparation, initiation or waging a war of aggression, or a war of violation of international treaties, agreements or assurances, or participation in a common plan or conspiracy for the accomplishment of any of the foregoing. (quoted in Heller 2011, 473)

War crimes and crimes against peace both concern violations that occur in reference to a war, but war crimes only *happen once a war has begun*, while a crime against peace *is the illegal initiation of a state of war in the first place*. As with war crimes, a crime against peace could be a single action within a genocide. For instance, one country might invade another with the intent of committing genocide. A modern example is Indonesia's invasion of East Timor in 1975, which occurred during the process of East Timor gaining independence from Portuguese colonial rule. The intention of the invasion was to subjugate the East Timorese and absorb them into Indonesia as Indonesian nationals, thereby destroying them as a distinct group on their own territory.

Examples are much more common in ancient times. One could go so far as to argue that the initiation of war in the ancient world was often genocidal in intent, as the final stage frequently involved the wholesale killing of the defeated group. For instance, Rome's explicit goal for the Third Punic War was to destroy Carthage, which it did, thereby completing a genocide that was initiated by a breach of peace.

Ethnic Cleansing: A Contested Term and Its Relationship to Genocide

Distinguishing "genocide" from "ethnic cleansing" is more complex than differentiating genocide from the three terms just treated above, because "ethnic cleansing" itself is a contested term. Unlike "genocide," "crimes against humanity," "war crimes," and "crimes against peace," "ethnic cleansing" is neither a legally defined term nor a specifically illegal act. Moreover, because of its origin as a euphemism for mass violence introduced by perpetrators in the former Yugoslavia, some scholars and others see it as tainted. Yet the term is used by scholars and others in various contexts and has indeed been used as a concept in legal decisions. In the paragraph that follows, we offer an account of "ethnic cleansing" in its usual usage, and then explain its relationship to genocide.

In what has emerged as its most common usage, "ethnic cleansing" constitutes the forced displacement of people of a specific ethnic or religious group from an area they occupy. The end goal of the perpetrators is to create a homogenous population in the region or nation from which the people are being expelled. Ethnic cleansing can be accomplished in various ways, including but not limited to: killing members of the targeted group; inflicting violence—such as rape—designed to drive out direct victims and other members of the group; chasing members of the targeted group away from the region through the threat of violence; and physically rounding up and deporting members of the targeted group. Ethnic cleansing often includes subsequent destruction of evidence of the targeted group's existence in the region, including places of worship, schools, civic buildings, libraries, flags, and so on.

As with crimes against humanity, ethnic cleansing can be genocidal. If a perpetrator purposely uses ethnic cleansing techniques with the intent to destroy a group in whole or in part, then this is a case of genocide. That actually was the case, for example, in Darfur, Sudan, when the Government of Sudan attempted to exterminate the black Africans of Darfur. To accomplish this, the GoS carried out aerial attacks against the villages of the black Africans with Antonov bombers and launched ground attacks by Janjaweed militia and GoS troops in Land Cruisers. In the process, the perpetrators raped girls and women that they caught on their farms or in their *tukuls* (homes). Upon an attack, most villagers fled from their homes out into the desert, nearby *wadis* (rivers that run during the rainy season and are dry for the rest of the year), and up into the mountains. The perpetrators would frequently throw dead donkeys or people in village wells, thus poisoning the water. They did so on the assumption that some of the people who fled might return to their villages upon the perpetrators' departure, and would, sooner or later, drink the water in the well. But having poisoned the well, the perpetrators knew that those who drank the water would end up extremely sick, if not dead. The perpetrators would also either steal everything in sight or burn the village to the ground, along with the farms, thus leaving the black Africans with nothing to eat. The region is so forbidding that the perpetrators knew that leaving the survivors with poisoned well water, no crops, and no food stores would either force the people to leave the region or face death. Thus in order to eliminate the black African population of Darfur, the perpetrators drove them out of their home areas through ethnic cleansing. By creating difficult or impossible living situations by making the victims' former villages uninhabitable, the perpetrators deliberately imposed conditions of life calculated to bring about the physical destruction of the black African population of Darfur, and thus committed genocide in the process.

While an entire campaign of ethnic cleansing might be a genocide, perpetrators might make use of genocide as a tool within a larger conflict that is not genocide. For instance, the 1995 killing of some eight thousand Muslim boys and men at Srebrenica has been recognized by the International Court of Justice (ICJ) as a genocidal act that occurred in a broader campaign of violence and expulsion that the ICJ did *not* characterize as genocide but which appears clearly to fit the definition of ethnic cleansing.

Similarly, genocide often uses methods typical of ethnic cleansing. In the cases of Darfur, the Cambodian genocide, the Holocaust, and the Armenian genocide, targeted groups were forced out of their homes, villages, towns, and cities by perpetrators in order to rid the area of such groups of people. These cases were genocidal, and not merely ethnic cleansing, because of the intent of those deportations. In each case, the goal of the perpetrators was not simply to remove the target group from a given area of land but to destroy them in whole or part as a group through killing and other means during and after the deportations.

There is a further complexity that is especially relevant to Indigenous groups with strong ties to the land they inhabit. In such cases, a specific area of land, with its various natural and human-made features, including religious edifices, urban areas, and so on, functions as the medium through which members of a group have social ties and is a unique site of spiritual and cultural significance. For instance, a specific mountain, river, town, or other feature of a territory can be part of the identity of a group. These unique features cannot simply be exchanged for others, and thus such groups cannot simply be moved to new areas without potentially destroying them as groups—as evidenced by cases in which such dispersions have weakened or even led to the extinction of the identities of the groups moved, as has occurred in North America, for instance. Under such circumstances, a case can be made that forced removal—that is, ethnic cleansing—is genocidal.

The complex relationship between genocide and ethnic cleansing highlights the need for precision and caution when employing the latter term in a discussion of genocide. It is best to ask whether a case of forced displacement and mass violence fits the UNCG definition of genocide; if it does, the term "genocide" is appropriate. Conversely, describing such cases as "ethnic cleansing" is likely to cause unnecessary confusion or even be perceived as an attempt at denying that a genocide has occurred or is occurring. Only when a case clearly *does not* fit the definition of genocide *and* has the features of ethnic cleansing as delineated above should the latter term be used.

Conclusion

While this chapter is intended to make clear the sharp distinctions between genocide and other categories of mass violence or mass human rights violations, including ethnic cleansing, the reader should be prepared to come across the use of these terms in ways that do not observe the differences explained here. This can be very confusing, especially for students new to the study of genocide.

The term "genocide" has frequently been misapplied for purposes of propaganda or in an attempt by a perpetrator (and/or its allies) to downplay genocidal actions. For example, in 1995, as NATO carried out aerial strikes against Bosnian Serb military targets, Russia charged that the Serbs were facing genocide from the West. In fact, NATO was attempting to halt crimes against humanity, war crimes, and genocide being perpetrated by the Serbs.

Those new to the study of genocide can avoid confusion by gaining a precise knowledge of the UNCG definition of genocide as well as the definitions of crimes against humanity, war crimes, and ethnic cleansing.

References

Heller, Kevin John. 2011. *The Nuremberg Military Tribunals and the Origins of International Criminal Law*. New York: Oxford University Press.

International Committee of the Red Cross. n.d. "Rule 156. Serious Violations of International Humanitarian Law Constitute War Crimes." *IHL* [International Humanitarian Law] *Database, Customary IHL*. Accessed July 19, 2019. https://ihl-databases.icrc.org/customary-ihl/eng/docs/vi_cha_chapter44_rule156

International Military Tribunal. 1945. *Charter of the International Military Tribunal*. Nuremberg: International Military Tribunal.

Morgenthau, Henry. (1915) 2004. "Telegram from American Ambassador to Turkey to the Secretary of State in Washington, D.C., July 16, 1915." In *United States Official Records on the Armenian Genocide, 1915–1917*, compiled by Ara Sarafian. Reading, UK: Taderon Press/Gomidas Institute.

Sands, Philippe. 2010. "My Legal Hero: Hersch Lauterpacht." *The Guardian*, November 10. http://www.guardian.co.uk/law/2010/nov/10/my-legal-hero-hersch-lauterpacht

Schabas, William A. 2009. *Genocide in International Law*. 2nd ed. London: Cambridge University Press.

Theriault, Henry C. 2010. "Genocidal Mutation and the Challenge of Definition." *Metaphilosophy* 41 (4): 481–524.

Tomuschat, Christian. 2006. "The Legacy of Nuremberg." *Journal of International Criminal Justice* 4 (4): 830–44.

UN General Assembly. 1947. *General Assembly Resolution 177(II)* [Formulation of the principles recognized in the Charter of the Nürnberg Tribunal and in the judgment of the Tribunal]. November 21. A/RES/177(II). http://research.un.org/en/docs/ga/quick/regular/2

— 1998. *Rome Statute of the International Criminal Court*. United Nations, Treaty Series, Vol. 2187, No. 38544. July 17. http://research.un.org/en/docs/ga/quick/regular/2

United States Holocaust Memorial Museum. n.d. "Pogroms." *Holocaust Encyclopedia*. Accessed January 2, 2018. https://encyclopedia.ushmm.org/content/en/article/pogroms

5

Applications of the UNCG in Representative Cases of Genocide at the ICTR and ICTY

Since its inception, the United Nations Convention on the Prevention and Punishment of the Crime of Genocide (UNCG) has shaped the scholarly, political, and judicial understandings of and responses to genocide. For this reason, an introduction to the UNCG must include a discussion of its application in specific legal cases. In looking at legal applications of the term "genocide," it is critical to understand and appreciate the fact that courts (including the International Criminal Court and the International Court of Justice) and tribunals (such as the International Criminal Tribunal for Rwanda and the International Criminal Tribunal for the Former Yugoslavia) tend to be more conservative in their application of the UNCG than readers might believe appropriate given the actual text of the UNCG and the spirit underlying it (as presented in chapters 1 through 4). Scholars, political leaders, and others generally tend to be broader in their interpretations and applications, which are, at times, looked at askance by experts in international law. This tension is actually healthy.

Courts focus on the technical aspects of the UNCG and related laws in trying cases and making decisions, and cannot rely on political judgments or academic analyses to fill in gaps in evidence. While courts can exercise some power to shape the meaning of the UNCG through interpretation, they cannot make new laws or fix problems or fill gaps in existing laws. This is precisely what lawmakers, policy makers, and scholars can do: they can identify the limitations of law and attempt to bring the letter of the law into conformity with the ethical and political imperatives that should be the foundations and guides for all lawmaking. Furthermore, policy makers and scholars identify the points at which legal considerations must give way to political, social, and cultural initiatives and processes. While the legal system can work well for the prosecution of major individual perpetrators based on the UNCG, it is not—with very limited exceptions—designed to address the broader questions of societal responsibility for genocide or the appropriate means of restoring, as much as possible, a victim community after it has suffered genocide. In these contexts, the UNCG does not function as a law, but rather as an ethical foundation for political, social, and cultural engagement of the legacies of genocide. Similarly, the UNCG as law has limited use beyond the threat of prosecution; it is, rather, as a guide to policy that it has a significant potential to support genocide prevention.

Over forty-five years slid by between the ratification of the UNCG on 12 January 1951, and the first conviction of an individual for perpetrating genocide on 2 September 1998. During that time period, one genocide after another was perpetrated across the globe, including but not limited to the Bangladesh genocide (1971), the Cambodian genocide (1975–79), the Rwandan genocide (1994), and the genocide at Srebrenica (1995).

Other than Nazi perpetrators of the Holocaust, every perpetrator of genocide in the post–World War II period had enjoyed utter impunity. With the advent of the ICTR and ICTY, impunity, at least for some, came to an end. At the very least, the international community seemed intent on bringing to bear charges against the main planners, leaders, and overseers of genocides perpetrated in Rwanda in 1994 and the former Yugoslavia (Bosnia-Herzegovina) in 1995. Still later, with the establishment of the International Criminal Court, perpetrators of other genocides were put on notice that their destructive actions were not to go unpunished, if the court could help it.[20]

This chapter serves three primary purposes. First, it provides readers with insight as to how actual tribunals and courts have referenced and applied the UNCG in their deliberations in regard to whether a criminal act constitutes genocide or not. Second, it illustrates how actual tribunals and courts have referenced and applied the UNCG to decide whether a defendant is guilty of genocide or not. And, third, the chapter format is specifically arranged to encourage readers to apply the knowledge and analytical skills they have gained through study of chapters 1 through 4 to actual court cases. With the foundation from the earlier chapters, we believe readers are now in a position to determine whether they think a court was correct or incorrect in its final decision, and why or why not.

In a single chapter, we cannot hope to do justice to the various dimensions of the many cases in which the UNCG has been applied since the 1990s in the ICTR, ICTY, ICC, and other courts such as the ICJ. Our goal is more modest: to introduce readers to the role of the UNCG in legal proceedings. To this end, we focus on two important cases of the 1990s that laid key foundations for genocide case law since. While more recent cases have added subtleties and new aspects to the application of the UNCG in courts, these early cases provide excellent illustrations of how courts apply the UNCG and the challenges associated with doing so. Moreover, in the same way that understanding the subtleties of recent civil rights cases in the United States requires familiarity with such landmark cases as *Dred Scott v. Sanford*, *Plessy v. Ferguson*, and *Brown v. Board of Higher Education of Topeka*, study of the *Akayesu* and *Krstić* cases is essential for understanding later applications of the UNCG. We are confident that students who work through this chapter carefully will be well-situated for study of further genocide cases adjudicated by the ICTY, ICTR, ICC, the ICJ, and other courts.

The decisions, arguments, and final judgments (all of which are available online) of the various Court Chambers at the ICTY, ICTR, ICC, and ICJ are often replete with detailed discussions as to whether a particular crime rises to the level of genocide versus some other criminal act, such as crimes against humanity. During the proceedings of such cases, various aspects of Article II of the UNCG are parsed, discussed, debated, and then often debated again in appeal hearings. Among some of the many issues that are often under the microscope, so to speak, are the following: the meaning of the term "intent," that which constitutes "in part" in the phrase "in whole or in part," whether a particular group targeted by the perpetrators actually constitutes a protected group under the UNCG, how the term "group" should be understood—"objectively" or "subjectively," the meaning of the phrase "as such," and so on. At the same time, various cases at the ICTR and ICTY have set precedents in international law in regard to how various terms in the UNCG and various actions by perpetrators (i.e., their words, decisions, actions, etc.) should be understood in case law as they relate to genocide, crimes against humanity, and ethnic cleansing.

International Criminal Tribunal for the Former Yugoslavia (ICTY)

The ICTY was established on 25 May 1993, and concluded its work on 21 December 2017. Established by the United Nations under Chapter VII of the UN Charter, the ICTY's express purpose was to deal with the crimes of an international nature that were committed during the conflicts in the Balkans throughout the 1990s: crimes against humanity, genocide, violations of the laws or customs of war, and grave breaches of the Geneva Conventions. It was based in The Hague.

During the course of its work, the ICTY indicted 161 individuals, sentenced ninety, acquitted nineteen, withdrew and/or terminated thirty-seven proceedings, referred thirteen for trial in various countries in the former Yugoslavia, and transferred two cases to other jurisdictions via the United Nations Mechanism for International Criminal Tribunals. On its website, the ICTY notes that, "while the most significant number of cases heard at the Tribunal have dealt with alleged crimes committed by Serbs and Bosnian Serbs, the Tribunal has investigated and brought charges against persons from every ethnic background. Convictions have been secured against Croats, as well as both Bosnian Muslims and Kosovo Albanians for crimes committed against Serbs and others" (ICTY n.d.a, para. 7).

The ICTY was the focus of a number of firsts in international law:

♦ It was the first war crimes court created by the United Nations (ICTY n.d.a, para. 2).
♦ It was first international war crimes tribunal to hear cases since the Nuremberg and Tokyo tribunals in the aftermath of World War II (ICTY n.d.a, para. 1).
♦ It specified crucial elements of the crime of genocide, in particular the definition of the target of genocide (ICTY n.d.b, para 37).
♦ It indicted, tried, and—when the facts supported the finding—found guilty individuals no matter what their positions were in society during the commission of the crimes, thus "dismantl[ing] the tradition of impunity for war crimes" (ICTY n.d.b, para. 1). The ICTY "indicted heads of state, prime ministers, army chiefs-of-staff, government ministers and many other leaders from various parties to the Yugoslav conflicts" (ICTY n.d.b, para. 1).
♦ It was the first international war crimes trial to consider charges of sexual violence (ICTY n.d.c, para. 6).[21]
♦ The Kunarac et al. judgment clearly defined rape as a tool of war. During the war in the former Yugoslavia, Dragoljub Kunarac was the

commander of a special volunteer unit of nonlocal irregular Serb soldiers mainly from Montenegro. He headed up a reconnaissance unit which formed part of the local Foca Tactical Group. The indictment against him covers "the brutal regime of gang-rape, torture and enslavement which Muslim women of Foca and elsewhere were subjected to between April 1992 and February 1993 by Bosnian Serb soldiers, policemen and members of paramilitary groups, including some coming from Serbia and Montenegro" (ICTY 1996).

The Trial Chamber at the ICTY found Kunarac guilty on eleven counts: one count of torture, a crime against humanity; three counts of rape, a crime against humanity; one count of enslavement, a crime against humanity; two counts of torture, a violation of the laws or customs of war; and four counts of rape, a violation of the laws or customs of war. He was sentenced to twenty-eight years in prison (ICTY 2002, 2–3).

♦ The Radislav Krstić case "established a link between rape and ethnic cleansing, which, in the context of Srebrenica crimes in July 1995, was closely associated with genocide" (ICTY n.d.c.).

♦ In the Anto Furundžija case, the Tribunal's judges confirmed that rape may be used as a tool of genocide, which had been established in a landmark precedent in 1998 when the ICTR judgment in the Akayesu case concluded, "With regard, particularly, to the acts described in paragraphs 12(A) and 12(B) of the Indictment, that is, rape and sexual violence, the Chamber wishes to underscore the fact that in its opinion, they constitute genocide in the same way as any other act as long as they were committed with the specific intent to destroy, in whole or in part, a particular group, targeted as such" (International Criminal Tribunal for Rwanda 1998, p. 176, para. 731). During the war in the former Yugoslavia, Bosnian Croat Anto Furundžija was a commander of a militia called the Jokers. On 10 December 1998, Trial Chamber II of the ICTY found Furundžija "guilty as a co-perpetrator of torture as a violation of the laws or customs of war," and "guilty as an aider and abettor of outrages upon personal dignity, including rape, as a violation of the laws or customs of war." Furundžija was sentenced to ten years of imprisonment for the first conviction and eight years of imprisonment for the second conviction (ICTY 1998, para. 1420).

- The ICTY "applied the modern doctrine of criminal responsibility of superiors, so-called command responsibility, thus clarifying that a formal superior-subordinate relationship is not necessarily required for criminal responsibility. In the same vein, the Tribunal removed uncertainty about the level of knowledge to be expected from a superior whose subordinates were about to commit crimes or actually committed them" (Lijun 2009, 359).

- For the first time in history, in 1999, an international criminal court charged a sitting head of state (Serbian President Slobodan Milošević) with international criminal acts.

As noted above, the ICTY's first conviction on the charge of genocide occurred when Radislav Krstić was found guilty of the genocide committed in 1995 in Srebrenica, Bosnia and Herzegovina. The conviction occurred in 2001.

Presented below is a significant section of the Judgment of the Appeals Chamber in the case of *Prosecutor v. Radislav Krstić*. The defense appealed several findings in the original judgment, including the issue as to whether it was accurate for the court to have found that *a substantial part of the group* of Bosnian Muslims in Srebrenica had actually been targeted and killed. The issues/meanings of both "in part" and "intent" were at the heart of the appeal.

While relatively lengthy, this excerpt from the Appeal Court is included here because it provides the reader with a solid sense as to the sort of give and take and attention to the smallest details that such discussions entail. Concomitantly, it provides readers with insight into the type of arguments that are made to support or dismiss a finding/decision by a Court Chamber. Ultimately, the transcript provides readers with a real-world glance into the workings of a court that was specifically established to try cases dealing with alleged instances of genocide and crimes against humanity.

The issue over what "in part" means in the UNCG is frequently a point of contention in genocide cases, and this particular Appeals Court does an excellent job of providing an explanation as to why it supports—and thus corroborates—the finding made in the original trial as to how "in part" should be understood. Likewise, it presents a very clear argument as to why it also agrees with the decision made in the original trial that genocide had been perpetrated against a substantive part of the people of Srebrenica. Following the excerpt from the document we present a short analysis of key points in relation to the Trial Chamber's discussion of various aspects of the UNCG.

Case No.: IT-98-33-A[22]

Date: 19 April 2004

Original:

English

IN THE APPEALS CHAMBER

Before: Judge Theodor Meron, Presiding

Judge Fausto Pocar

Judge Mohamed Shahabuddeen

Judge Mehmet Güney

Judge Wolfgang Schomburg

Registrar: Mr. Hans Holthuis

Judgement: 19 April 2004

PROSECUTOR

v.

RADISLAV KRSTIĆ

JUDGEMENT

Counsel for the Prosecution:

Mr. Norman Farrell

Mr. Mathias Marcussen

Ms. Magda Karagiannakis

Mr. Xavier Tracol

Mr. Dan Moylan

Counsel for the Defendant:

Mr. Nenad Petrušić

Mr. Norman Sepenuk

A. The Definition of the Part of the Group

6. Article 4 of the [ICTY's] Statute, like the Genocide Convention, covers certain acts done with "intent to destroy, in whole or in part, a national, ethnical, racial or religious group, as such." The Indictment in this case alleged, with respect to the count of genocide, that Radislav Krstić "intend[ed] to destroy a part of the Bosnian Muslim people as a national, ethnical, or religious group." The targeted group identified in the Indictment, and accepted by the Trial Chamber, was that of the Bosnian Muslims. The Trial Chamber determined that the Bosnian Muslims were a specific, distinct national group, and therefore covered by Article 4. This conclusion is not challenged in this appeal.

7. As is evident from the Indictment, Krstić was not alleged to have intended to destroy the entire national group of Bosnian Muslims, but only a part of that group. The first question presented in this appeal is whether, in finding that Radislav Krstić had genocidal intent, the Trial Chamber defined the relevant part of the Bosnian Muslim group in a way [that] comports with the requirements of Article 4 and of the Genocide Convention.

8. It is well established that where a conviction for genocide relies on the intent to destroy a protected group "in part," the part must be a substantial part of that group. The aim of the Genocide Convention is to prevent the intentional destruction of entire human groups, and the part targeted must be significant enough to have an impact on the group as a whole. Although the Appeals Chamber has not yet addressed this issue, two Trial Chambers of this Tribunal have examined it. In Jelisić, the first case to confront the question, the Trial Chamber noted that, "given the goal of the [Genocide] Convention to deal with mass crimes, it is widely acknowledged that the intention to destroy must target at least a *substantial* part of the group." The same conclusion was reached by the Sikirica Trial Chamber: "This part of the definition calls for evidence of an intention to destroy a substantial number relative to the total population of the group." As these Trial Chambers explained, the substantiality requirement both captures genocide's defining character as a crime of massive proportions and reflects the Convention's concern with the impact the destruction of the targeted part will have on the overall survival of the group.

9. The question has also been considered by Trial Chambers of the ICTR, whose Statute contains an identical definition of the crime of

genocide. These Chambers arrived at the same conclusion. In *Kayishema*, the Trial Chamber concluded, after having canvassed the authorities interpreting the Genocide Convention, that the term "'in part' requires the intention to destroy a considerable number of individuals who are part of the group." This definition was accepted and refined by the Trial Chambers in *Bagilishema* and *Semanza*, which stated that the intent to destroy must be, at least, an intent to destroy a substantial part of the group.

10. This interpretation is supported by scholarly opinion. The early commentators on the Genocide Convention emphasized that the term "in part" contains a substantiality requirement. Raphael Lemkin, a prominent international criminal lawyer who coined the term "genocide" and was instrumental in the drafting of the Genocide Convention, addressed the issue during the 1950 debate in the United States Senate on the ratification of the Convention. Lemkin explained that "destruction in part must be of a substantial nature so as to affect the entirety." He further suggested that the Senate clarify, in a statement of understanding to accompany the ratification, that "the Convention applies only to actions undertaken on a mass scale." ...

12. The intent requirement of genocide under Article 4 of the Statute is therefore satisfied where evidence shows that the alleged perpetrator intended to destroy at least a substantial part of the protected group. The determination of when the targeted part is substantial enough to meet this requirement may involve a number of considerations. The numeric size of the targeted part of the group is the necessary and important starting point, though not in all cases at the ending point of the inquiry. The number of individuals targeted should be evaluated not only in absolute terms, but also in relation to the overall size of the entire group. In addition to the numeric size of the targeted portion, its prominence within the group can be a useful consideration. If a specific part of the group is emblematic of the overall group, or is essential to its survival, that may support a finding that the part qualifies as substantial within the meaning of Article 4.

13. The historical examples of genocide also suggest that the area of the perpetrators' activity and control, as well as the possible extent of their reach, should be considered. Nazi Germany may have intended only to eliminate Jews within Europe alone; that ambition probably did not extend, even at the height of its power, to an undertaking of that enterprise on a global scale. Similarly, the perpetrators of genocide in Rwanda did not seriously contemplate the elimination of the Tutsi population beyond the country's borders. The intent to destroy formed by a perpetrator of genocide will always be limited by the opportunity presented to him. While this factor

alone will not indicate whether the targeted group is substantial, it can—in combination with other factors—inform the analysis.

14. These considerations, of course, are neither exhaustive nor dispositive. They are only useful guidelines. The applicability of these factors, as well as their relative weight, will vary depending on the circumstances of a particular case.

15. In this case, having identified the protected group as the national group of Bosnian Muslims, the Trial Chamber concluded that the part the VRS [the Army of Republika Srpska] Main Staff and Radislav Krstić targeted was the Bosnian Muslims of Srebrenica, or the Bosnian Muslims of Eastern Bosnia. This conclusion comports with the guidelines outlined above. The size of the Bosnian Muslim population in Srebrenica prior to its capture by the VRS forces in 1995 amounted to approximately forty thousand people. This represented not only the Muslim inhabitants of the Srebrenica municipality but also many Muslim refugees from the surrounding region. Although this population constituted only a small percentage of the overall Muslim population of Bosnia and Herzegovina at the time, the importance of the Muslim community of Srebrenica is not captured solely by its size. As the Trial Chamber explained, Srebrenica (and the surrounding Central Podrinje region) were of immense strategic importance to the Bosnian Serb leadership. Without Srebrenica, the ethnically Serb state of Republika Srpska they sought to create would remain divided into two disconnected parts, and its access to Serbia proper would be disrupted. The capture and ethnic purification of Srebrenica would therefore severely undermine the military efforts of the Bosnian Muslim state to ensure its viability, a consequence the Muslim leadership fully realized and strove to prevent. Control over the Srebrenica region was consequently essential to the goal of some Bosnian Serb leaders of forming a viable political entity in Bosnia, as well as to the continued survival of the Bosnian Muslim people. Because most of the Muslim inhabitants of the region had, by 1995, sought refuge within the Srebrenica enclave, the elimination of that enclave would have accomplished the goal of purifying the entire region of its Muslim population.

16. In addition, Srebrenica was important due to its prominence in the eyes of both the Bosnian Muslims and the international community. The town of Srebrenica was the most visible of the "safe areas" established by the UN Security Council in Bosnia. By 1995 it had received significant attention in the international media. In its resolution declaring Srebrenica a safe area, the Security Council announced that it "should be free from armed attack or any other hostile act." This guarantee of protection was re-affirmed by the commander of the UN Protection Force in Bosnia

(UNPROFOR) and reinforced with the deployment of UN troops. The elimination of the Muslim population of Srebrenica, despite the assurances given by the international community, would serve as a potent example to all Bosnian Muslims of their vulnerability and defenselessness in the face of Serb military forces. The fate of the Bosnian Muslims of Srebrenica would be emblematic of that of all Bosnian Muslims.

17. Finally, the ambit of the genocidal enterprise in this case was limited to the area of Srebrenica. While the authority of the VRS Main Staff extended throughout Bosnia, the authority of the Bosnian Serb forces charged with the take-over of Srebrenica did not extend beyond the Central Podrinje region. From the perspective of the Bosnian Serb forces alleged to have had genocidal intent in this case, the Muslims of Srebrenica were the only part of the Bosnian Muslim group within their area of control.

18. In fact, the Defence does not argue that the Trial Chamber's characterization of the Bosnian Muslims of Srebrenica as a substantial part of the targeted group contravenes Article 4 of the Tribunal's Statute. Rather, the Defence contends that the Trial Chamber made a further finding, concluding that the part Krstić intended to destroy was the Bosnian Muslim men of military age of Srebrenica. In the Defence's view, the Trial Chamber then engaged in an impermissible sequential reasoning, measuring the latter part of the group against the larger part (the Bosnian Muslims of Srebrenica) to find the substantiality requirement satisfied. The Defence submits that if the correct approach is properly applied, and the military age men are measured against the entire group of Bosnian Muslims, the substantiality requirement would not be met.

19. The Defence misunderstands the Trial Chamber's analysis. The Trial Chamber stated that the part of the group Radislav Krstić intended to destroy was the Bosnian Muslim population of Srebrenica. The men of military age, who formed a further part of that group, were not viewed by the Trial Chamber as a separate, smaller part within the meaning of Article 4. Rather, the Trial Chamber treated the killing of the men of military age as evidence from which to infer that Radislav Krstić and some members of the VRS Main Staff had the requisite intent to destroy all the Bosnian Muslims of Srebrenica, the only part of the protected group relevant to the Article 4 analysis.

20. In support of its argument, the Defence identifies the Trial Chamber's determination that, in the context of this case, "the intent to kill the men [of military age] amounted to an intent to destroy a substantial part of the Bosnian Muslim group." The Trial Chamber's observation was proper. As a specific intent offense, the crime of genocide requires proof of intent to commit the underlying act and proof of intent to destroy the targeted group, in whole or in part. The proof of the mental state with respect to

the commission of the underlying act can serve as evidence from which the fact-finder may draw the further inference that the accused possessed the specific intent to destroy.

21. The Trial Chamber determined that Radislav Krstić had the intent to kill the Srebrenica Bosnian Muslim men of military age. This finding is one of intent to commit the requisite genocidal act—in this case, the killing of the members of the protected group, prohibited by Article 4(2)(a) of the Statute. From this intent to kill, the Trial Chamber also drew the further inference that Krstić shared the genocidal intent of some members of the VRS Main Staff to destroy a substantial part of the targeted group, the Bosnian Muslims of Srebrenica....

23. The Trial Chamber's determination of the substantial part of the protected group was correct. The Defence's appeal on this issue is dismissed.

The above excerpt from the Appeals Chamber of the Krstić case provides unique insights into how prosecutors, defense teams, and judges weigh, discuss, debate, and posit counterarguments vis-à-vis key terms and concepts found in the UNCG. When such terms are argued about in a court, the discussion is no longer academic; a defendant's entire future is on the line, not to mention the prospects for a sense of justice for surviving members of victims' families and the victim group in general, which itself could influence the likelihood of a peaceful post-genocide transition. The reasoning presented to support court decisions can even determine the extent to which such decisions are accepted by other members of the perpetrator group, which is another factor affecting the chance of a peaceful post-genocide transition.

In this case, this relatively short excerpt (the entire transcript is 155 pages) from the Judgment of the Appeals Court addresses three significant points in relation to the UNCG: (1) how the concept of "in part" should be understood, (2) how the concept of "*substantial* part" should be understood, and (3) why the mass murder of Bosnian Muslim males in Srebrenica constituted a "substantial part" of the group as a whole. Here, the fate of the defendant and its influence on the broader process of post-genocide transition made interpretation of terminology much more than the academic exercise it might otherwise appear to be.

What is particularly fascinating is how the defense attempts to extricate Krstić from responsibility for the tragedy at Srebrenica by claiming that he was falsely charged with and found guilty of genocide as a result of the prosecutor and court's incorrect interpretation as to what constituted a "substantial part" of the Bosnian Muslim population in the region. In doing so, the defense argued "that if the correct approach [had been] properly applied, and the military age men [were] measured against the entire group of Bosnian Muslims, the substantiality requirement would not be met." The prosecutor and judges, though, had already countered this argument by referencing several other cases at the ICTY, as well as those of the Holocaust and the ICTR, and then asserted that "the elimination of that enclave [the UN designated 'safe area' at Srebrenica, where some forty-thousand Bosnian Muslims had sought sanctuary from the killing] would have accomplished the goal of purifying the entire region of its Muslim population."

What we, the readers, glean from the Court's argument is not only the significance of the issue of "substantive" but a history lesson in regard to how the differing sides (Serbs vs Bosnian Muslims) perceived the significance of their presence in the region. In the Court's words, "control over the Srebrenica region was consequently essential to the goal of some Bosnian Serb leaders of forming a viable political entity in Bosnia, as well as to the continued survival of the Bosnian Muslim people."

In regard to the Appeal Court's assertion that both the number of Bosnian Muslim men killed as well as the argument that the men were "essential to the group's survival," Payam Akhavan (2012), professor of International Law at McGill University in Montreal, made the following observations:

ICTY jurisprudence includes ... both a quantitative and a qualitative criterion. Of course, the qualitative criterion—with its assumption that a group's leaders may be central to a group's viability—involves implicitly and arguably controversial judgments as to the relative worth of the group's "ordinary" members.

Another important qualification in the definition of genocide is that genocidal intent may be confined to a limited geographic zone or, as stipulated by the ICJ, it "is not necessary to intend to achieve the complete annihilation of a group from every corner of the globe.... The ICTY noted that, even though the Bosnian Muslims of Srebrenica and the eastern enclaves comprised only a 'small' percentage' of the overall Muslim population of Bosnia, 'the import of the community is not appreciated solely by its size' and that the Srebrenica enclave was of immense strategic importance to the Bosnian Serb leadership," etc.

... This analysis, albeit persuasive, shows just how many complex judgments may have to be made about the social, cultural, political and economic aspects of a given situation. (48–49)

The Appeals Court also concurred with the Trial Chamber that it was evident that Krstić acted with "intent." According to the Court, "the Trial Chamber determined that Radislav Krstić had the intent to kill the Srebrenica Bosnian Muslim men of military age. This finding is one of intent to commit the requisite genocidal act—in this case, the killing of the members of the protected group, prohibited by Article 4(2)(a) of the Statute" (see para. 21 above).

Radislav Krstić was sentenced to forty-six years imprisonment, but the ICTY Appeals Chamber reduced the sentence to thirty-five years, with credit for time already served: "In the light of the circumstances of this case, as well as the nature of the grave crimes Radislav Krstić has aided and abetted or committed, the Appeals Chamber, taking into account the principle of proportionality, consider[ed] that the sentence imposed by the Trial Chamber should be reduced to 35 years" (ICTY 2004, para. 275).

Some may ask why the death penalty was not considered in this case, but the fact is the death penalty was not on the table as an option at either the ICTY or the ICTR. The reason why the death penalty was not an option is largely due, it seems, to the fact that an ever-increasing number of nations across the globe, especially in Europe, reject the death penalty as an acceptable punishment under any circumstances. As Olin (2005) has put it,

> many human rights lawyers took for granted that an emerging norm of international law forbade the use of the death penalty in all circumstances, even for the extreme crime of genocide. This view prevailed among the European powers on the Security Council, any one of which could exercise its veto to block empowering a tribunal to impose capital punishment. Just as the permissibility of the death penalty was considered so obvious at Nuremberg that no serious discussion of the matter was required, so its impermissibility was now considered so obvious that once again no serious debate ensued. When the ICTR and then the ICTY were created, the death penalty was officially off the table. (748)

International Criminal Tribunal for Rwanda (ICTR)

On 8 November 1994, the UN Security Council established the ICTR, an international criminal tribunal expressly for the prosecution of persons allegedly responsible for genocide, crimes against humanity, "and other serious violations of international humanitarian law committed on the territory of Rwanda and neighbouring States, between 1 January 1994 and 31 December 1994. The Tribunal [was] located in Arusha, Tanzania, and [had] offices in Kigali, Rwanda" (UN International Residual Mechanism for Criminal Tribunals n.d.a, para. 2). Its Appeals Chamber was located in The Hague, the Netherlands.

The ICTR completed its work in December 2015. Over the course of its operation it indicted ninety-three individuals for genocide and other serious violations of international humanitarian law committed in Rwanda during the one hundred days of the genocide (7 April–4 July 1994). Two of its indictments were withdrawn; upon being tried, fourteen individuals were acquitted; two alleged *genocidaires* died prior to being found guilty or innocent; twenty-three of those found guilty served their full sentences; six died before or while serving their sentences; thirty-three were transferred to various states to serve their sentences; and five were transferred to other jurisdictions (three to Rwanda and two to France). An additional eight fugitive cases were transferred to other jurisdictions via the United Nations Mechanism for International Criminal Tribunals (UN International Residual Mechanism for Criminal Tribunals n.d.b, paras. 2–3).

Like the ICTY, the work of the ICTR resulted in a number of firsts in international criminal law. The ICTR was the first international criminal tribunal to:

♦ Enter a judgment for genocide (Akayesu trial; UN International Residual Mechanism for Criminal Tribunals n.d.a, para. 5).
♦ "Interpret the definition of genocide set forth in the 1948 Geneva Conventions" (Akayesu trial; UN International Residual Mechanism for Criminal Tribunals n.d.a, para. 5).
♦ "Define rape in international criminal law" (Akayesu trial; UN International Residual Mechanism for Criminal Tribunals n.d.a, para. 5).
♦ "Recognise rape as a means of perpetrating genocide" (Akayesu trial; UN International Residual Mechanism for Criminal Tribunals n.d.a, para. 5).
♦ Hold that a conviction for "complicity of genocide" required proof that the defendant actually participated in the killing (Akayesu trial; Malone 2008, 216).
♦ Hold that "direct, public incitement to commit genocide [which Akayesu did] is a crime that carries personal criminal liability" (Akayesu trial; Malone 2008, 216).
♦ Have an accused person admit responsibility for committing genocide, conspiracy to commit genocide, and crimes against humanity. (The former Interim Government Prime Minister Jean Kambanda pled guilty to genocide.)
♦ Issue a judgment (the first since Nuremberg) against a former head of state.
♦ Hold members of the media responsible for broadcasts aimed at inciting the public to commit acts of genocide. (In the same case, the Media Case,[23] the Appeals Chamber confirmed that the legal doctrine of superior responsibility applies to civilians in leadership positions.)

♦ Indict and arrest a woman (i.e., former Family Affairs Minister Pauline Nyiramasuhuko).

♦ Convict the first woman (former Family Affairs Minister Pauline Nyiramasuhuko) ever charged with genocide. She was found guilty of genocide, conspiracy to commit genocide, and rape as a crime against humanity.

One of the most notorious and now famous cases heard by the ICTR was the Akayesu case. The defendant, Jean-Paul Akayesu, who was the *bourgmestre* (mayor) of a small town called Taba prior to and during the genocide, was ultimately convicted on nine counts of genocide and crimes against humanity for his role in the deaths of two thousand Tutsis who had sought his protection. While he asserted he had no power to halt the killings, one judge hearing the case, Judge Laity Kama, stated that Akayesu was "individually and criminally responsible for the deaths." In the end, Akayesu was sentenced to life in prison. He was sentenced to an additional eighty years for other crimes, including rape (see ICTR 1998).

In the following excerpt from the Judgment in the Trial Chamber in the Akayesu trial, readers glean insights into how the Trial Chamber interpreted the definition of genocide and how the concept of genocide applied or did not apply to what occurred in Rwanda between 6 April 1994 and 4 July 1994. Again, this case was (and is) particularly significant in light of the fact that the Akayesu case was the first case to result in a conviction for genocide. It should be noted that much of what is stated in this excerpt is repeated from what had been addressed and established early on in the trial, which is the protocol in judgment hearings.

CHAMBER I - CHAMBRE I

OR : ENG

Before:

Judge Laïty Kama, Presiding

Judge Lennart Aspegren

Judge Navanethem Pillay

Registry:

Mr. Agwu U. Okali

Decision of: 2 September 1998

THE PROSECUTOR

VERSUS

JEAN-PAUL AKAYESU

Case No. ICTR-96-4-T

JUDGEMENT

The Office of the Prosecutor:

Mr. Pierre-Richard Prosper

Counsel for the Accused:

Mr. Nicolas Tiangaye

Mr. Patrice Monthé

...

3. GENOCIDE IN RWANDA IN 1994?

112. As regards the massacres which took place in Rwanda between April and July 1994 ..., the question before this Chamber is whether they constitute genocide. Indeed, it was felt in some quarters that the tragic events which took place in Rwanda were only part of the war between the Rwandan Armed Forces (the RAF) and the Rwandan Patriotic Front (RPF). The answer to this question would allow a better understanding of the context within which the crimes with which the accused is charged are alleged to have been committed.

113. According to paragraph 2 of Article 2 of the Statute of the Tribunal, which reflects verbatim the definition of genocide as contained in the Convention on the Prevention and Punishment of the Crime of Genocide (hereinafter, "the Convention on Genocide"), genocide means any of the following acts referred to in said paragraph, committed with intent to destroy, in whole or in part, a national, ethnical, racial or religious group as such, namely, *inter alia*: killing members of the group; causing serious bodily or mental harm to members of the group.

114. Even though the number of victims is yet to be known with accuracy, no one can reasonably refute the fact that widespread killings were perpetrated throughout Rwanda in 1994.

115. Indeed, this is confirmed by the many testimonies heard by this Chamber. The testimony of Dr. Zachariah who appeared before this Chamber on 16 and 17 January 1997 is enlightening in this regard. Dr. Zachariah was a physician who at the time of the events was working for a non-governmental organisation, "Médecins sans frontières." In 1994 he was based in Butare and travelled over a good part of Rwanda up to its border with Burundi. He described in great detail the heaps of bodies which he saw everywhere, on the roads, on the footpaths and in rivers and, particularly, the manner in which all these people had been killed. At the church in Butare, at the Gahidi mission, he saw many wounded persons in the hospital who, according to him, were all Tutsi and who, apparently, had sustained wounds inflicted with machetes to the face, the neck, and also to the ankle, at the Achilles' tendon, to prevent them from fleeing. The testimony given by Major-General Dallaire, former Commander of the United Nations Assistance Mission for Rwanda (UNAMIR) at the time of the events alleged in the Indictment, who was called by the defence, is of a similar vein. Major-General Dallaire spoke of troops of the Rwandan Armed Forces and of the Presidential Guard going into houses in Kigali that had been previously identified in order to kill ...

116. The British cameraman, Simon Cox, took photographs of bodies in many churches in Remera, Biambi, Shangi, between Cyangugu and Kibuye, and in Bisesero. He mentioned identity cards strewn on the ground, all of which were marked "Tutsi." Consequently, in view of these widespread killings the victims of which were mainly Tutsi, the Chamber is of the opinion that the first requirement for there to be genocide has been met, the killing and causing serious bodily harm to members of a group.

117. The second requirement is that these killings and serious bodily harm, as is the case in this instance, be committed with the intent to destroy, in whole or in part, a particular group targeted as such.

118. In the opinion of the Chamber, there is no doubt that considering their undeniable scale, their systematic nature and their atrociousness, the massacres were aimed at exterminating the group that was targeted. Many facts show that the intention of the perpetrators of these killings was to cause the complete disappearance of the Tutsi. In this connection, Alison Desforges [sic],[24] an expert witness, in her testimony before this Chamber on 25 February 1997, stated as follows: "On the basis of the statements made by certain political leaders, on the basis of songs and slogans popular among the Interahamwe, I believe that these people had the intention of completely wiping out the Tutsi from Rwanda so that—as they said on certain occasions—their children, later on, would not know what a Tutsi looked like,

unless they referred to history books." Moreover, this testimony given by Dr. Desforges was confirmed by two prosecution witnesses, witness KK and witness OO, who testified separately before the Tribunal that one Silas Kubwimana had said during a public meeting chaired by the accused himself [Akayesu] that all the Tutsi had to be killed so that someday Hutu children would not know what a Tutsi looked like.

119. Furthermore, as mentioned above, Dr. Zachariah also testified that the Achilles' tendons of many wounded persons were cut to prevent them from fleeing. In the opinion of the Chamber, this demonstrates the resolve of the perpetrators of these massacres not to spare any Tutsi. Their plan called for doing whatever was possible to prevent any Tutsi from escaping and, thus, to destroy the whole group. Witness OO further told the Chamber that during the same meeting, a certain Ruvugama, who was then a Member of Parliament, had stated that he would rest only when no single Tutsi is left in Rwanda.

120. Dr. Alison Desforges testified that many Tutsi bodies were often systematically thrown into the Nyabarongo River, a tributary of the Nile. Indeed, this has been corroborated by several images shown to the Chamber throughout the trial. She explained that the underlying intention of this act was to "send the Tutsi back to their place of origin," to "make them return to Abyssinia," in keeping with the allegation that the Tutsi are foreigners in Rwanda, where they are supposed to have settled following their arrival from the Nilotic regions.

121. Other testimonies heard, especially that of Major-General Dallaire, also show that there was an intention to wipe out the Tutsi group in its entirety, since even newborn babies were not spared. Even pregnant women, including those of Hutu origin, were killed on the grounds that the foetuses in their wombs were fathered by Tutsi men, for in a patrilineal society like Rwanda, the child belongs to the father's group of origin. In this regard, it is worthwhile noting the testimony of witness PP, heard by the Chamber on 11 April 1997, who mentioned a statement made publicly by the accused [Akayesu] to the effect that if a Hutu woman were impregnated by a Tutsi man, the Hutu woman had to be found in order "for the pregnancy to be aborted." ...

122. In light of the foregoing, it is now appropriate for the Chamber to consider the issue of specific intent that is required for genocide (*mens rea* or *dolus specialis*). In other words, it should be established that the above-mentioned acts were targeted at a particular group as such. In this respect also, many consistent and reliable testimonies, especially those of Major-General Dallaire, Dr. Zachariah, victim V, prosecution witness

PP, defence witness DAAX, and particularly that of the accused himself [Akayesu] unanimously agree on the fact that it was the Tutsi as members of an ethnic group which they formed in the context of the period in question, who were targeted during the massacres.

123. Two facts, in particular, which suggest that it was indeed the Tutsi who were targeted should be highlighted: Firstly, at the roadblocks which were erected in Kigali immediately after the crash of the President's plane on 6 April 1994 and, later on, in most of the country's localities, members of the Tutsi population were sorted out. Indeed, at these roadblocks which were manned, depending on the situation, either by soldiers, troops of the Presidential Guard and/or militiamen, the systematic checking of identity cards indicating the ethnic group of their holders, allowed the separation of Hutu from Tutsi, with the latter being immediately apprehended and killed, sometimes on the spot. Secondly, the propaganda campaign conducted before and during the tragedy by the audiovisual media, for example, "Radio Television des MilleCollines" (RTLM), or the print media, like the *Kangura* newspaper. These various news media overtly called for the killing of Tutsi, who were considered as the accomplices of the RPF and accused of plotting to take over the power lost during the revolution of 1959. Some articles and cartoons carried in the *Kangura* newspaper, entered in evidence, are unambiguous in this respect. In fact, even exhibit 25A could be added to this lot. Exhibit 25A is a letter ... dated 21 September 1992 and signed by Deofratas Nsabimana, Colonel, BEM, to which is annexed a document prepared by a committee of ten officers and which deals with the definition of the term enemy. According to that document, which was intended for the widest possible dissemination, the enemy fell into two categories, namely: "the primary enemy" and the "enemy supporter." The primary enemy was defined as "the extremist Tutsi within the country or abroad who are nostalgic for power and who have NEVER acknowledged and STILL DO NOT acknowledge the realities of the Social Revolution of 1959, and who wish to regain power in RWANDA by all possible means, including the use of weapons."[25] On the other hand, the primary enemy supporter was "anyone who lent support in whatever form to the primary enemy" ...

124. In the opinion of the Chamber, all this proves that it was indeed a particular group, the Tutsi ethnic group, which was targeted. Clearly, the victims were not chosen as individuals but, indeed, because they belonged to said group; and hence the victims were members of this group selected as such. According to Alison Desforges's testimony, the Tutsi were killed solely on account of having been born Tutsi.[26]

125. Clearly therefore, the massacres which occurred in Rwanda in 1994 had a specific objective, namely the extermination of the Tutsi, who were targeted especially because of their Tutsi origin and not because they were RPF fighters. In any case, the Tutsi children and pregnant women would, naturally, not have been among the fighters.

126. Consequently, the Chamber concludes from all the foregoing that genocide was, indeed, committed in Rwanda in 1994 against the Tutsi as a group. Furthermore, in the opinion of the Chamber, this genocide appears to have been meticulously organized. In fact, Dr. Alison Desforges testifying before the Chamber on 24 May 1997, talked of "centrally organized and supervised massacres." Indeed, some evidence supports this view that the genocide had been planned. First, the existence of lists of Tutsi to be eliminated is corroborated by many testimonies. In this respect, Dr. Zachariah mentioned the case of patients and nurses killed in a hospital because a soldier had a list including their names. There are also the arms caches in Kigali which Major-General Dallaire mentioned and regarding whose destruction he had sought the UN's authorization in vain. Lastly, there is the training of militiamen by the Rwandan Armed Forces and of course, the psychological preparation of the population to attack the Tutsi, which preparation was masterminded by some news media, with the RTLM at the forefront....

5. FACTUAL FINDINGS

171. Moreover, customary rules existed in Rwanda governing the determination of ethnic group, which followed patrilineal lines of heredity. The identification of persons as belonging to the group of Hutu or Tutsi (or Twa) had thus become embedded in Rwandan culture. The Rwandan witnesses who testified before the Chamber identified themselves by ethnic group, and generally knew the ethnic group to which their friends and neighbours belonged. Moreover, the Tutsi were conceived of as an ethnic group by those who targeted them for killing.

172. As the expert witness, Alison Desforges, summarised:

The primary criterion for [defining] an ethnic group is the sense of belonging to that ethnic group. It is a sense which can shift over time. In other words, the group, the definition of the group to which one feels allied may change over time. But, if you fix any given moment in time, and you say, how does this population divide itself, then you will see which ethnic groups are in existence in the minds of the participants at that time. The Rwandans currently, and for the last generation at least, have defined themselves in terms of these three ethnic groups. In addition reality is an interplay between the actual conditions and peoples' subjective perception of those conditions. In Rwanda, the reality was shaped by the colonial experience which imposed a categorisation which was probably more fixed, and not completely appropriate to the scene. But, the Belgians did impose this classification in the early 1930's when they required the population to be registered according to ethnic group. The categorisation imposed at that time is what people of the current generation have grown up with. They have always thought in terms of these categories, even if they did not, in their daily lives have to take cognizance of that. This practice was continued after independence by the First Republic and the Second Republic in Rwanda to such an extent that this division into three ethnic groups became an absolute reality.

This excerpt provides a fascinating and instructive view into how one Trial Chamber at the ICTR actually went about assessing whether a defendant should be brought up on charges of crimes against humanity, genocide, or something else altogether. Slowly but surely the Trial Chamber, in its Judgment phase, addresses specific evidence provided by eyewitnesses in order to make a determination as to which group or groups had been under attack, the type of injuries and abuses perpetrated against the victims, the evidence that supports the intent to destroy in whole or in part, and so on.

First, the issue of groups is discussed. Among the evidence collected by the Trial Chamber as to whether the people were killed as individuals or as part of a group, the evidence presented here supports the determination that they were, in fact, targeted as members of a group, Tutsis:

♦ At the church in Butare, at the Gahidi mission, he [a witness for the prosecution] saw many wounded persons in the hospital who, according to him, were all Tutsi and who, apparently, had sustained wounds inflicted with machetes to the face, the neck, and also to the ankle, at the Achilles' tendon, to prevent them from fleeing.

♦ The testimony given by Major-General Dallaire, former Commander of the United Nations Assistance Mission for Rwanda (UNAMIR) at the time of the events alleged in the Indictment, who was called by the defence, is of a similar vein. Major-General Dallaire spoke of troops of the Rwandan Armed Forces and of the Presidential Guard going into houses in Kigali that had been previously identified in order to kill.

♦ The British cameraman, Simon Cox, took photographs of bodies in many churches in Remera, Biambi, Shangi, between Cyangugu and Kibuye, and in Bisesero. He mentioned identity cards strewn on the ground, all of which were marked "Tutsi." *Consequently, in view of these widespread killings the victims of which were mainly Tutsi, the Chamber is of the opinion that the first requirement for there to be genocide has been met, the killing and causing serious bodily harm to members of a group* (emphasis added).

Second, the Trial Chamber provides a very clear rationale as to how and why it established that the perpetrators during the mass killing between 6 April and 4 July 1994, had the intent to destroy, in whole or in part, a particular group, as such (in this case, the Tutsis of Rwanda). Among the comments of the witnesses and other evidence heard by the Trial Chamber in regard to the issue of intent are the following:

♦ Many facts show that the intention of the perpetrators of these killings was to cause the complete disappearance of the Tutsi. In this connection, Alison Desforges [*sic*], an expert witness, in her testimony before this Chamber on 25 February 1997, stated as follows: "On the basis of the statements made by certain political leaders, on the basis of songs and slogans popular among the *Interahamwe*, I believe that these people had the intention of completely wiping out the Tutsi from Rwanda so that— as they said on certain occasions—their children, later on, would not know what a Tutsi looked like, unless they referred to history books."

♦ Moreover, the testimony given by Dr. Desforges was confirmed by two prosecution witnesses, witness KK and witness OO, who testified separately before the Tribunal that one Silas Kubwimana had said during a public meeting chaired by the accused himself [Akayesu] that all the Tutsi had to be killed so that someday Hutu children would not know what a Tutsi looked like.

♦ Furthermore, as mentioned above, Dr. Zachariah also testified that the Achilles' tendons of many wounded persons were cut to prevent them from fleeing. In the opinion of the Chamber, this demonstrates the resolve of the perpetrators of these massacres not to spare any Tutsi. Their plan called for doing whatever was possible to prevent any Tutsi from escaping and, thus, to destroy the whole group.[27]

♦ Witness OO further told the Chamber that during the same meeting, a certain Ruvugama, who was then a Member of Parliament, had stated that he would rest only when no single Tutsi is left in Rwanda.

♦ Other testimonies heard, especially that of Major-General Dallaire, also show that there was an intention to wipe out the Tutsi group in its entirety, since even newborn babies were not spared. Even pregnant women, including those of Hutu origin, were killed on the grounds that the foetuses in their wombs were fathered by Tutsi men, for in a patrilineal society like Rwanda, the child belongs to the father's group of origin.

♦ It is worthwhile noting the testimony of witness PP, heard by the Chamber on 11 April 1997, who mentioned a statement made publicly by the accused [Akayesu] to the effect that if a Hutu woman were impregnated by a Tutsi man, the Hutu woman had to be found in order "for the pregnancy to be aborted."

The issue of specific intent (*mens rea* or *dolus specialis*) was also clearly established by the Trial Chamber and the subsequent Appeals Chamber in relation to the same (Akayesu) case. Again, what follows are the comments of the witnesses and discussion of the other evidence heard by the Trial Chamber in regard to the issue of specific intent (i.e., proof that the criminal acts were targeted at a particular group, as such):

♦ Many consistent and reliable testimonies, especially those of Major-General Dallaire, Dr. Zachariah, victim V, prosecution witness PP, defence witness DAAX, and particularly that of the accused himself [Akayesu] unanimously agree on the fact that it was the Tutsi as members of an ethnic group which they formed in the context of the period in question, who were targeted during the massacres.

♦ At the roadblocks which were erected in Kigali immediately after the crash of the President's plane on 6 April 1994 and, later on, in most of the country's localities, members of the Tutsi population were sorted out. Indeed, at these roadblocks which were manned, depending on the situation, either by soldiers, troops of the Presidential Guard and/or militiamen, the systematic checking of identity cards indicating the ethnic group of their holders, allowed the separation of Hutu from Tutsi, with the latter being immediately apprehended and killed, sometimes on the spot.

♦ The propaganda campaign conducted before and during the tragedy by the audiovisual media, for example, "Radio Television des Mille Collines" (RTLM), or the print media, like the *Kangura* newspaper ... overtly called for the killing of Tutsi.

♦ Exhibit 25A is a letter ... dated 21 September 1992 and signed by Deofratas Nsabimana, Colonel, BEM, to which is annexed a document prepared by a committee of ten officers and which deals with the definition of the term enemy. According to that document, which was intended for the widest possible dissemination, the enemy fell into two categories, namely: "the primary enemy" and the "enemy supporter." The primary enemy was defined as "the extremist Tutsi within the country or abroad who are nostalgic for power and who have NEVER acknowledged and STILL DO NOT acknowledge the realities of the Social Revolution of 1959, and who wish to regain power in RWANDA by all possible means, including the use of weapons." On the other hand, the primary enemy supporter was "anyone who lent support in whatever form to the primary enemy."

The Trial Chamber states that, "in the opinion of the Chamber, all this proves that it was indeed a particular group, the Tutsi ethnic group, which was targeted. Clearly, the victims were not chosen as individuals but, indeed, because they belonged to said group; and hence the victims were members of this group selected as such."

Subsequently, the Chamber concludes from the evidence available to it, including the foregoing, "that genocide was, indeed, committed in Rwanda in 1994 against the Tutsi as a group. Furthermore, in the opinion of the Chamber, this genocide appears to have been meticulously organized."

Conclusion

Reading and analyzing the records of actual trials at the ICTR and ICTY is often quite revelatory. Doing so provides one with unique insights into how jurists carefully consider, weigh, and debate the meaning of various terms found in the UNCG's definition of genocide in relation to a case under consideration. One might think that the meaning and understanding of such terms would have been settled by now, some seventy years since the advent of the UNCG. Obviously, that is not the case. Then again, as legal scholars note, case law is always evolving.

Such records present unique and powerful views into real-life applications of terms, with the fates of the defendants hanging in the balance. They provide readers with a bird's-eye view, if you will, of the real-life application of such terms.

Hopefully readers now appreciate why it is so worthwhile to seek out, read, and examine the actual case histories and testimony presented at the ICTR and ICTY hearings. This is one of the best ways to ascertain how court chambers wrestle with issues and come to key determinations, including whether or not a defendant is guilty of genocide, and on what grounds and why.

References

Akhavan, Payam. 2012. *Reducing Genocide to Law: Definition, Meaning, and the Ultimate Crime.* New York: Cambridge University Press.

Human Rights Watch. 2009. "Human Rights Watch Mourns Loss of Alison Des Forges: Leading Rwanda Expert Killed in Plane Crash." February 13. https://www.hrw.org/news/2009/02/13/human-rights-watch-mourns-loss-alison-des-forges

International Criminal Tribunal for Rwanda. 1998. *Prosecutor v. Jean-Paul Akayesu.* Case No. ICTR-96-4-T, Judgment (Trial Chamber), September 2. Arusha, Tanzania.

International Criminal Tribunal for the Former Yugoslavia. n.d.a. "About the ICTY." Accessed January 2, 2018, http://www.icty.org/en/about

— n.d.b. "Achievements." Accessed January 2, 2018, http://www.icty.org/en/about/tribunal/achievements

— n.d.c. "Landmark Cases." Accessed January 2, 2018, http://www.icty.org/en/features/crimes-sexual-violence/landmark-cases

International Criminal Tribunal for the Former Yugoslavia. 1996. "Gang Rape, Torture and Enslavement of Muslim Women Charged in ICTY's First Indictment Dealing Specifically with Sexual Offences." Press release. CC/PIO/093-E. June 27. http://www.icty.org/en/sid/7334

— 2004. *Prosecutor v. Radislav Krstić.* Case No. IT-98-33-A, Judgment (Appeals Chamber), April 19. The Hague.

Lijun, Yang. 2009. "ICTY." In *The Oxford Companion to International Criminal Justice,* edited by Antonio Cassese, 357–59. London: Oxford University Press.

Malone, Linda A. 2008. *Emmanuel Law Outlines.* New York: Aspen Publishers.

Olin, Jens David. 2005. "Applying the Death Penalty to Crimes of Genocide." *American Journal of International Law* 99 (4): 747–77.

Rugiririza, Ephrem. 2015. "Historic Decisions of the ICTR." JusticeInfo.net. November 30. https://www.justiceinfo.net/en/tribunals/ictr/526-historic-decisions-of-the-ictr.html

United Nations International Residual Mechanism for Criminal Tribunals. n.d.a. "ICTR in Brief." Accessed January 2, 2018, http://unictr.irmct.org/en/tribunal

— n.d.b. "Key Figures of Cases." Accessed January 2, 2018, http://unictr.irmct.org/en/cases/key-figures-cases

Conclusion

Those who have carefully read this book and discussed or debated the numerous issues addressed in it should have acquired the knowledge:

♦ to conduct more accurate and advanced study of and research into the issue of genocide, including the ability to read and interpret legal decisions making use of the UNCG;
♦ to engage in knowledgeable discussions about how the UNCG's definition of genocide establishes key criteria and major limitations in regard to what is deemed genocide under the purview of international law;
♦ to assess whether contemporary atrocities constitute crimes against humanity, war crimes, or genocide;
♦ to make accurate and insightful appraisals of the validity of observations, assertions, and decisions issued by courts, the United Nations, individual governments, and the media vis-à-vis contemporary atrocities;
♦ to present measured arguments justifying their positions based on a precise understanding of the UNCG and related issues;
♦ to engage in knowledgeable discussion about how the UNCG definition might be too limited or, conversely, too broad;
♦ to engage in knowledgeable discussion about how the UNCG definition of genocide might be updated, and why and how; and
♦ to take an active and significant part in future discussions with family members, colleagues, and friends about the UNCG and the issue of genocide.

To be equipped to undertake the abovementioned activities is to have a unique power. It provides one with the means to keep the United Nations, individual countries (or at least one's own), and the media honest. This can be accomplished in a host of ways, including for example, via:

♦ letters to the editor or guest commentaries and editorial pieces in national (e.g., *The New York Times*, *The Wall Street Journal*, or *The Washington Post*), regional, state, or local newspapers;
♦ appearances on local, regional, or national media broadcasts;
♦ blogs entries, Facebook posts, tweets, and other communications to small or large audiences through social media;
♦ letters to and meetings with political leaders, such as representatives in the US Congress; and
♦ organizing or participating in concerned citizen groups, public gatherings, and rallies, and so on

Furthermore, such skills can be carried forward into one's future activities, whether these include, for example, working for an investment house or sitting as a judge or on a jury. When a genocide occurs in a specific region of the world where financial companies have investments, critical decisions must be made about withdrawing or not withdrawing assets controlled by the perpetrators. A judge and a jury may well be called on to decide a case in which a former perpetrator of genocide has gained residency in the US through falsification of his/her/their past. An investor in a mutual fund might be asked to vote in favor of or against a company that continues to do business in a nation where the government is perpetrating genocide. Understanding what genocide is and the law around it allows an individual in such situations to "do the right thing" and to help others do so as well.

While some of these ideas might seem quite remote from the lives of various readers now, it should be noted that many of the most effective people on the issue of genocide—starting with Raphael Lemkin himself, right through to the students of STAND: The Student-Led Movement to End Mass Atrocities—initially addressed their concerns and focused their attention on matters outside of the realm of professional life, while gradually reaching larger and larger audiences and higher and higher levels of authority.

Far too often in the past and present, various individuals and groups have recklessly, mindlessly, or lazily referred to one situation or another as genocide when it plainly was not. All too often, activists, the media, and even educators at the university level seem to consider any major human rights violation as constituting genocide.

Others have callously, ignorantly, or lazily failed to recognize that violence constituted genocide when it did. The classic case, of course, is the 1994 genocide perpetrated in Rwanda by radical Hutus and their compatriots against the Tutsi and moderate Hutu. Countless witnesses, including those with the power to intervene, continued throughout the one hundred days of killing to resist acknowledging that genocide, not a mutual civil war, was occurring, which, to their way of thinking, allowed them to stand by and do nothing.

Still others have made claims that such matters as abortions (regardless of whether the fetus is considered a full person or not) constitute genocide, despite the fact that, whatever one's views of these issues may be, they are not genocides according to a reasonable application of the UN definition.

With newly acquired, in-depth knowledge of the United Nations Convention on the Prevention and Punishment of the Crime of Genocide, readers are now in a position to evaluate claims of genocide accurately and objectively and to render well-reasoned judgments. They are also in a position to recognize whether a genocide is being perpetrated despite political leaders' and journalists' avoidance of the term. That is a means by which to set the record straight in a profoundly meaningful way. The importance of the role readers can now assume cannot be overestimated. Each and every individual can make a difference in calling attention to an emerging genocide and spur action against it, which has the potential to save thousands and more lives. This is true power.

The authors hope that, beyond supporting readers in developing this range of knowledge relative to genocide and the UNCG specifically, this book has convinced readers that genocide should not only be an issue of concern to each and every one of us, but an issue that committed individuals can influence. Perhaps some readers will be enticed by their study of the nuances of genocide law presented in this book to consider law school and a legal career through which they will one day sit on a genocide tribunal. Others might bring an understanding of genocide into their study of and careers in business, public health, criminal justice, psychology, philosophy, religion, education, political science, sociology, anthropology, women's studies, global studies, or history.

If we have helped readers gain a clearer, more exact understanding of what genocide is and the main legal mechanisms used to address it, then we have accomplished what we set out to do. This is also true if we have equipped the reader with a greater sense of confidence to delve into the study of genocide, to take part in classroom discussions of issues that relate to actual or potential genocides, and to make reasoned statements (be it in the classroom, in written assignments, or in discussions with friends or family members) about a case of, for example, mass murder, based on their understanding of the UNCG.

Selected Preparatory Documents
(in Chronological Order)

General Assembly Resolution 96 (I) of 11 December 1946 (The Crime of Genocide)
Economic and Social Council Resolution 47 (IV) of 28 March 1947 (Crime of
Genocide) (E/437 [E/325])
Draft convention on the crime of genocide prepared by the Secretary-General in
pursuance of the Economic and Social Council resolution 47 (IV) (E/447, 26
June 1947)
Economic and Social Council Resolution 77 (V) of 6 August 1947 (Genocide)
Note by the Secretary-General, Draft Convention on the Crime of Genocide
(A/362, 25 August 1947)
General Assembly Resolution 180 (II) of 21 November 1947 (Draft convention on
genocide)
Economic and Social Council Resolution 117 (VI) of 3 March 1948 (Genocide)
Report of the Ad Hoc Committee on Genocide and draft Convention drawn up by
the Committee, 5 April to 10 May 1948 (E/794)
Sixth Committee of the General Assembly, Summary records of meetings nos.
63 to 66 held from 30 September to 4 October 1948 (A/C. 6/SR. 63, 64, 65,
and 66)
Report of the Drafting Committee, "Genocide: Draft convention and Report of the
Economic and Social Council" (A/C.6/288, 23 November 1948)
Sixth Committee of the General Assembly, Summary records of meetings nos. 67
to 69, 71 to 87, 91 to 110, and 128 to 134, held, respectively, from 5 to 7 October,
11 to 29 October, 4 to 18 November, and 29 November to 2 December 1948
(A/C.6/SR. 67, 68, 69, 71, 72, 73, 74, 75, 76, 77, 78, 79, 80, 81, 82, 83, 84, 85,
86, 87, 91, 92, 93, 94, 95, 96, 97, 98, 99, 100, 101, 102, 103, 104, 105, 106, 107, 108,
109, 110, 128, 129, 130, 131, 132, 133, and 134)
Report of the Sixth Committee of the General Assembly, "Genocide: Draft convention and Report of the Economic and Social Council" (A/760 and Corr.2,
3 December 1948 and 6 December 1948, respectively)

General Assembly, Verbatim records of plenary meetings nos. 178 and 179 held on 9 December 1948 (A/PV. 178 and 179)

General Assembly Resolution 260 (III) of 9 December 1948 (Prevention and Punishment of the Crime of Genocide)

The United Nations Convention on the Prevention and Punishment of the Crime of Genocide

Adopted by Resolution 260 (III) A of the United Nations General Assembly on 9 December 1948.

Article I

The Contracting Parties confirm that genocide, whether committed in time of peace or in time of war, is a crime under international law which they undertake to prevent and to punish.

Article II

In the present Convention, genocide means any of the following acts committed with intent to destroy, in whole or in part, a national, ethnical, racial or religious group, as such:

(a) Killing members of the group;
(b) Causing serious bodily or mental harm to members of the group;
(c) Deliberately inflicting on the group conditions of life calculated to bring about its physical destruction in whole or in part;
(d) Imposing measures intended to prevent births within the group;
(e) Forcibly transferring children of the group to another group.

Article III

The following acts shall be punishable:

(a) Genocide;
(b) Conspiracy to commit genocide;

(c) Direct and public incitement to commit genocide;
(d) Attempt to commit genocide;
(e) Complicity in genocide. .

Article IV

Persons committing genocide or any of the other acts enumerated in Article 3 shall be punished, whether they are constitutionally responsible rulers, public officials or private individuals.

Article V

The Contracting Parties undertake to enact, in accordance with their respective Constitutions, the necessary legislation to give effect to the provisions of the present Convention and, in particular, to provide effective penalties for persons guilty of genocide or any of the other acts enumerated in Article 3.

Article VI

Persons charged with genocide or any of the other acts enumerated in Article 3 shall be tried by a competent tribunal of the State in the territory of which the act was committed, or by such international penal tribunal as may have jurisdiction with respect to those Contracting Parties which shall have accepted its jurisdiction.

Article VII

Genocide and the other acts enumerated in Article 3 shall not be considered as political crimes for the purpose of extradition.

The Contracting Parties pledge themselves in such cases to grant extradition in accordance with their laws and treaties in force.

Article VIII

Any Contracting Party may call upon the competent organs of the United Nations to take such action under the Charter of the United Nations as they consider appropriate for the prevention and suppression of acts of genocide or any of the other acts enumerated in Article 3.

Article IX

Disputes between the Contracting Parties relating to the interpretation, application or fulfilment of the present Convention, including those relating to the responsibility of a State for genocide or any of the other acts enumerated in Article 3, shall be submitted to the International Court of Justice at the request of any of the parties to the dispute.

Article X

The present Convention, of which the Chinese, English, French, Russian and Spanish texts are equally authentic, shall bear the date of 9 December 1948.

Article XI

The present Convention shall be open until 31 December 1949 for signature on behalf of any Member of the United Nations and of any non-member State to which an invitation to sign has been addressed by the General Assembly.

The present Convention shall be ratified, and the instruments of ratification shall be deposited with the Secretary-General of the United Nations.

After 1 January 1950, the present Convention may be acceded to on behalf of any Member of the United Nations and of any non-member State which has received an invitation as aforesaid.

Instruments of accession shall be deposited with the Secretary-General of the United Nations.

Article XII

Any Contracting Party may at any time, by notification addressed to the Secretary-General of the United Nations, extend the application of the present Convention to all or any of the territories for the conduct of whose foreign relations that Contracting Party is responsible.

Article XIII

On the day when the first twenty instruments of ratification or accession have been deposited, the Secretary-General shall draw up a proces-verbal and transmit a copy of it to each Member of the United Nations and to each of the non-member States contemplated in Article 11.

The present Convention shall come into force on the ninetieth day following the date of deposit of the twentieth instrument of ratification or accession.

Any ratification or accession effected subsequent to the latter date shall become effective on the ninetieth day following the deposit of the instrument of ratification or accession.

Article XIV

The present Convention shall remain in effect for a period of ten years as from the date of its coming into force.

It shall thereafter remain in force for successive periods of five years for such Contracting Parties as have not denounced it at least six months before the expiration of the current period.

Denunciation shall be effected by a written notification addressed to the Secretary-General of the United Nations.

Article XV

If, as a result of denunciations, the number of Parties to the present Convention should become less than sixteen, the Convention shall cease to be in force as from the date on which the last of these denunciations shall become effective.

Article XVI

A request for the revision of the present Convention may be made at any time by any Contracting Party by means of a notification in writing addressed to the Secretary-General.

The General Assembly shall decide upon the steps, if any, to be taken in respect of such request.

Article XVII

The Secretary-General of the United Nations shall notify all Members of the United Nations and the non-member States contemplated in Article 11 of the following:

(a) Signatures, ratifications and accessions received in accordance with Article 11;
(b) Notifications received in accordance with Article 12;
(c) The date upon which the present Convention comes into force in accordance with Article 13;
(d) Denunciations received in accordance with Article 14;
(e) The abrogation of the Convention in accordance with Article 15;
(f) Notifications received in accordance with Article 16.

Article XVIII

The original of the present Convention shall be deposited in the archives of the United Nations.

A certified copy of the Convention shall be transmitted to all Members of the United Nations and to the non-member States contemplated in Article 11.

Article XIX

The present Convention shall be registered by the Secretary-General of the United Nations on the date of its coming into force.

3 | List of Crimes against Humanity

The International Criminal Court and the Rome Statute

The permanent International Criminal Court, which came into force in 2002, offers another, slightly different definition of crimes against humanity from the account given in chapter 4. In its founding treaty, the Rome Statute, crimes against humanity are defined as follows:

For the purpose of this Statute, "crimes against humanity" means any of the following acts when committed as part of a widespread or systematic attack directed against any civilian population, with knowledge of the attack:

(a) Murder;
(b) Extermination;
(c) Enslavement;
(d) Deportation or forcible transfer of population;
(e) Imprisonment or other severe deprivation of physical liberty in violation of fundamental rules of international law;
(f) Torture;
(g) Rape, sexual slavery, enforced prostitution, forced pregnancy, enforced sterilization, or any other form of sexual violence of comparable gravity;
(h) Persecution against any identifiable group or collectivity on political, racial, national, ethnic, cultural, religious, gender as defined in paragraph 3, or other grounds that are universally recognized as impermissible under international law, in connection with any act referred to in this paragraph or any crime within the jurisdiction of the Court;
(i) Enforced disappearance of persons;
(j) The crime of apartheid;
(k) Other inhumane acts of a similar character intentionally causing great suffering, or serious injury to body or to mental or physical health.

4

The Responsibility to Protect (a Summary)

United Nations   A/63/677

General Assembly   Distr.: General

                                      12 January 2009

                                    Original: English

Sixty-third session

Implementing the Responsibility to Protect

Report of the Secretary-General

Summary

The present report responds to one of the cardinal challenges of our time, as posed in paragraphs 138 and 139 of the 2005 World Summit Outcome: operationalizing the responsibility to protect (widely referred to as "RtoP" or "R2P" in English). The Heads of State and Government unanimously affirmed at the Summit that "each individual State has the responsibility to protect its populations from genocide, war crimes, ethnic cleansing and crimes against humanity." They agreed, as well, that the international community should assist States in exercising that responsibility and in building their protection capacities. When a State nevertheless was "manifestly failing" to protect its population from the four specified crimes and violations, they confirmed that the international community was prepared to take collective action in a "timely and decisive manner" through the Security Council and in accordance with the Charter of the United Nations. As the present report underscores, the best way to discourage States or groups of States from misusing the responsibility to protect for inappropriate purposes would be to develop fully the United Nations strategy, standards, processes, tools and practices for the responsibility to protect.

This mandate and its historical, legal and political context are addressed in section I of the present report.

A three-pillar strategy is then outlined for advancing the agenda mandated by the Heads of State and Government at the Summit, as follows:

Pillar one

The protection responsibilities of the State (sect. II)

Pillar two

International assistance and capacity-building (sect. III)

Pillar three

Timely and decisive response (sect. IV)

... The strategy stresses the value of prevention and, when it fails, of early and flexible response tailored to the specific circumstances of each case. There is no set sequence to be followed from one pillar to another, nor is it assumed that one is more important than another. Like any other edifice, the structure of the responsibility to protect relies on the equal size, strength and viability of each of its supporting pillars. The report also provides examples of policies and practices that are contributing, or could contribute, to the advancement of goals relating to the responsibility to protect under each of the pillars.*

---

*   For the complete document, go to https://www.un.org/en/genocideprevention/about
-responsibility-to-protect.shtml and click on the link for "The Responsibility to Protect."

Notes

1 Ultimately, his birthplace would become known as Volkovysk in the nation of Belarus.
2 The use of "ethnocide" can be confusing. As noted by Barbra (2007), the original meaning of "ethnocide" as used by Lemkin was as an equivalent of genocide. The shift to cultural or identity destruction without necessarily physical destruction came later.
3 The Nuremberg Military Tribunal was the international court established by the victorious Allies after World War II to try high-ranking Germans who were involved in the planning and execution of the crimes perpetrated by Nazi Germany.
4 For a detailed discussion of Lemkin's affiliation with the International Military Tribunal at Nuremberg, see Barrett (2010).
5 For a detailed discussion of these issues as well as others, including but not limited to the issue of states' rights and the ratification of the UNCG and the fear that US citizens (particularly US troops) being tried for genocide would be tried in the state where the alleged crimes were committed rather than in the US, see LeBlanc (1991).
6 First emerging in the fifteenth century, the usage of "ethnical" was popular from the sixteenth to the nineteenth century. "Ethnical" is a synonym for "ethnic," and since "ethnic" is more commonly used today, we have chosen to use it throughout the book.
7 In this chapter, the text of the Convention itself is italicized, and the commentaries are in regular type. The preamble and all articles are included in full.
8 Based on a general understanding of each of the concepts/terms (i.e., racial, ethnical, religious, and national) in 1948, the following listing is an example of what such a breakdown looks like:

   ♦ *Racial Groups* (e.g., Asian, Black, Caucasian or White, or Australasian),

♦ *Ethnical Groups* (e.g., Arabs, Basques, Berbers, Bosniaks, Catalans, Gujarati, Hispanic or Latino, Kurds, Mongols, Pashtuns, Tamils),
♦ *Religious Groups* (e.g., adherents of Buddhism, Christianity, Confucianism, Judaism, Islam, Hinduism, Sikhism, etc.), and
♦ *National Groups* (e.g., Bolivian, English, French, Italian, Japanese, Russian, American, etc.).

9 Information drawn from interviews Sam Totten conducted during the US State Department's atrocities documentation project along the Darfur border.

10 The principle of "state sovereignty" stipulates that no external entity— another country or an international organization—can interfere in a country's internal matters.

11 Another way of understanding specific intent is to approach it in the following way: Article II of the Genocide Convention introduces a precise description in regard to that which the perpetrator *intends* to do. That precise description is the *intent "to destroy, in whole or in part, a national, ethnical, racial or religious group, as such."* As Schabas (2009) duly notes,

> The reference to "intent" … indicates that [those prosecutors, for example, engaged in trying defendants on the charge of genocide] must go beyond establishing that the offender meant to engage in the conduct, or meant to cause the consequence. The offender must also be proven to have a *"specific intent"* or *dolus specialis* [again, the intent to destroy in whole or in part, a racial, ethnic, national or religious group, as such]. Where the specified intent is not established, the acts remains punishable, but not as genocide. It may be classified as a crime against humanity or it may be simply a crime under ordinary criminal law. (257)

12 That is not to say that there are no documents associated with the genocidal process, but these documents typically misrepresent the actions being taken and the reasons they are being taken. For instance, a government might couch genocidal violence in terms of a reaction to a "rebel" insurgency or a civil war.

13 At the ICTR, the *Prosecutor v. Akayesu* (International Criminal Tribunal for Rwanda 1998) found the accused guilty of genocide under Article 2(2)(b) of the Statute of the International Criminal Tribunal for Rwanda (ICTR Statute), asserting that "rapes resulted in physical and psychological destruction of Tutsi women, their families and their communities. Sexual violence was an integral part of the process of destruction, specifically targeting Tutsi women and specifically contributing to their destruction and to the destruction of the Tutsi group as a whole" (para. 731). The trial chamber also found that the acts of rape and sexual violence resulted in serious bodily harm to members of the Tutsi group and were committed with the intent to destroy, in whole or in part, that same group.

Another ICTR judgment, *Prosecutor v. Muhimana* (International Criminal Tribunal for Rwanda 2005), found the accused guilty of rape as a crime against humanity (para. 585).

14 A disagreement continues to this day whether genocide was actually committed or not, with scholars debating whether the atrocities perpetrated rose to the level of genocide.

15 From the 1870s through the late twentieth century, it was widely and firmly believed that the native inhabitants of the island of Tasmania off the coast of Australia had been extinguished by the 1870s. Early works in genocide studies even echoed this belief. However, in recent decades, many individuals who trace their heritage to these earlier Tasmanians have come forward. Despite the longstanding belief to the contrary, the group was, in fact, destroyed only "in part."

16 Former Guatemala dictator Efrain Rios Montt "was found guilty for his role in the killings in May 2013. His eighty-year jail sentence was thrown out less than two weeks later, however, by Guatemala's Constitutional Court on a legal technicality after persistent efforts by Rios Montt's defense team to derail the trial with complex appeals" (Reuters 2016, paras. 5–6). "A retrial of Rios Montt on charges of genocide and crimes against humanity was suspended again for the court to resolve outstanding legal petitions, a judge said," on 11 January 2016 (para. 1). According to the court, "Rios Montt did not attend because of mental incapacity'" (para. 3).

17 Euphemisms such as "deportation," "liquidation," and even "ethnic cleansing" have been used by perpetrators before and after 1944, but are not our concern herein because they either misrepresent the genocidal process (e.g., both deportation and ethnic cleansing, for example, can be used as methods of committing genocide, but in and of themselves are not genocidal) or present genocide in inaccurate terms.

18 The Nazis used pogroms as part of the process both leading up to and in the execution of the Holocaust, but, in and of themselves, the pogroms were not genocides, per se, but rather components of a genocide (United States Holocaust Memorial Museum n.d.).

19 For the full text of The Hague conventions, see the International Committee of the Red Cross website: Convention (II) with Respect to the Laws and Customs of War on Land and Its Annex: Regulations Concerning the Laws and Customs of War on Land, https://ihl-databases.icrc.org /ihl/INTRO/150?OpenDocument; Convention (IV) Respecting the Laws and Customs of War on Land and Its Annex: Regulations Concerning the Laws and Customs of War on Land, https://ihl-databases.icrc.org /applic/ihl/ihl.nsf/385ec082b509e76c41256739003e636d/1d1726425f6955a ec125641e0038bfd6.

20 With the exception of the 1994 genocide in Rwanda, however, the vast majority of the killers responsible for the Srebrenica genocide and everyone (leaders, planners, killers) responsible for the Darfur genocide in Sudan and the Yazidi genocide in Iraq have enjoyed impunity. Still, a beginning is a beginning: the climate of impunity has at least shifted. If nothing else, most governments agree in theory that impunity must end for those who have committed genocide. What is needed now is the impetus for the individual

and collective members of the international community to act on that sentiment.

21 In that regard, the ICTY asserts that it "proved to the world that the nascent international criminal justice system could end impunity for sexual crimes and that punishing perpetrators was possible" (ICTY n.d.c, para. 6).

22 Readers can access the transcripts of the cases (ranging from the indictments, the hearings of both the original court cases and, where applicable, appeal hearings) heard at the ICTY and ICTR online. In doing so, readers will be privy to the actual words, discussions, and debates of the judges, prosecutors, defense attorneys, defendants, and witnesses, both in support of the prosecution and in support of the defense. In many instances, audiovisual portions of the actual hearings are available as well. These are remarkable resources that should not be overlooked. The official websites of the ICTY and ICTR are, respectively, http://www.icty.org/ and http://unictr.irmct.org/.

23 As for the Media Case, the ICTR was the "first international tribunal to hold members of the media responsible for broadcasts intended to inflame the public to commit acts of genocide" (UN International Residual Mechanism for Criminal Tribunals n.d.a, para. 6). On 3 December 2003, numerous individuals were found guilty of various charges for their role in using radio programming to incite genocide. Ferdinand Nahimana, one of the founders of Radio Télévision Libre des Mille Collines (RTLM), was found to be responsible, and thus guilty, for RTLM broadcasts inciting genocide—primarily for failing to prevent those under him from broadcasting such spurious information, for failing to punish them for having done so, and for failing to prevent them from broadcasting additional programs once he became aware of them, "whereas he knew or had reasons to know that they were committing crimes" (Rugiririza 2015, para. 4). "Hassan Ngeze, owner and director of the newspaper *Kangura*," was convicted in 1994 for inciting genocide through articles published in his newspaper. Both Nahimana and Ngeze received life sentences (Rugiririza 2015, para. 4). On appeal, in November 2007, both sentences were reduced: Nahimana's sentence was reduced to thirty years, and Ngeze's to thirty-five years (Rugiririza 2015, para. 4).

24 Alison Des Forges, a US citizen, was a historian and noted human rights activist whose work focused on Rwanda. For nearly two decades, up through 1999, at which time she sadly suffered an untimely death in an airplane accident in the US, Des Forges was a senior adviser to Human Rights Watch's Africa division. She was widely recognized as the leading expert on the 1994 Rwanda Genocide and its aftermath. As Kenneth Roth, the Executive Director of Human Rights Watch, said upon her death, "She was among the first to highlight the ethnic tensions that led to the genocide, and when it happened and the world stood by and watched, Alison did everything humanly possible to save people. Then she wrote the definitive account" (Human Rights Watch 2009, para. 2).

25 This is a reference to the Rwandan Patriotic Force (RPF).

26 Later in this case, the Appeal Chambers judgment of Akayesu duly reported the following:

> Regarding Akayesu's acts and utterances during the period relating to the acts alleged in the Indictment, the Chamber was satisfied beyond reasonable doubt, on the basis of all evidence brought to its attention during the trial, that on several occasions the accused made speeches calling, more or less explicitly, for the commission of genocide. The Chamber, in particular, held in its findings on Count 4, that the accused incurred individual criminal responsibility for the crime of direct and public incitement to commit genocide. Yet, according to the Chamber, the crime of direct and public incitement to commit genocide lies in the intent to directly lead or provoke another to commit genocide, which implies that he who incites to commit genocide also has the specific intent to commit genocide: that is, to destroy, in whole or in part, a national, ethnical, racial or religious group, as such. (International Criminal Tribunal for Rwanda 1998, para. 729)

27 The killers chased down victims one after another. They would sever an individual's Achilles tendons by hacking at them with a machete or *panga*, and leave the victim writhing on the ground as the perpetrators chased down more victims, repeating the same butchery over and over again. Once no other victims were in the vicinity to chase down, the killers went back and finished off those victims who had been injured to the extent that they could not run and hide.

Select Annotated Bibliography

General

Albright, Madeleine K., and William S. Cohen (chairs). 2008. *Preventing Genocide: A Blueprint for US Policymakers*. Washington, DC: Genocide Prevention Task Force. 147 pp.

Often referred to as the "Albright-Cohen Report" in honor of the co-chairs of the committee that wrote it, this report assesses the obstacles to effective prevention of and intervention against genocide by the United States. Some of the many issues it examines are the importance of leadership, particularly by the US president, ways of strengthening interagency cooperation within the US government, how to improve early warning and prevention efforts, and diplomatic and military approaches to potential and actual genocides. Its strongest aspect is the presentation of substantive recommendations regarding each of the avenues it discusses (leadership, early warning, etc.).

The Summer 2009 issue of *Genocide Studies and Prevention* (vol. 4, issue 2) contains a set of articles evaluating the Albright-Cohen Report, with a number that point out important problems with and flaws of the report, including Daniel Feierstein's "Getting Things into Perspective."

Barnett, Michael. 2003. *Eyewitness to a Genocide: The United Nations and Rwanda*. Ithaca, NY: Cornell University Press. 240 pp.

This is an important and well-written analysis by Michael Barnett, who served with the US Mission to the United Nations from 1993 to 1994. It is also a highly disturbing work, and one that should give pause to anyone who is concerned with the prevention of and intervention against genocide. Based on his experiences at the UN, interviews with key actors, and archival work, Barnett provides a sobering assessment of how and why the UN and its constituent departments reacted to the unfolding of the 1994 genocide in Rwanda. As

Barnett clearly and convincingly argues, "in the weeks leading up to the geno-cide, the UN was increasingly aware or had good reason to suspect that Rwanda was a site of crimes against humanity and yet it failed to act." Possibly most disturbing is that Barnett concludes that the UN's "indifference was driven not by incompetence or cynicism but rather by reasoned choices cradled by moral considerations." The book raises a host of key issues and concerns in regard to the United Nations' commitment to the UNCG.

Chalk, Frank, and Kurt Jonassohn. 1990. *The History and Sociology of Genocide: Analyses and Case Studies*. New Haven, CT: Yale University Press. 461 pp.

This was a groundbreaking text for genocide education. Its primary focus is the discussion and analysis of numerous case studies of genocide spanning human history. The book's introduction is worthy of special attention in that the authors offer a useful account of the genesis of the concept of genocide and the UNCG, followed by a thorough analysis (through 1990) of the literature on the definition of genocide. The authors discuss various perceived limitations of the UNCG and attempt to improve on its definition of genocide. The authors present a profoundly important proposal for addressing once and for which groups should be covered by the UNCG and how they should be defined. In doing so, they convincingly argue that it is, in fact, the perpetrators' definition of a target group that should be the standard against which the issues of intent and destruction are measured.

Evans, Gareth, and Mohamed Sahnoun. 2001. *The Responsibility to Protect: The Report of the International Commission on Intervention and State Sovereignty*. Ottawa: International Development Research Centre. 91 pp.

This important text argues that there exists under international law a "respon-sibility to protect" (often abbreviated as "R2P")—that is, an obligation by state governments to protect the human rights of all within their borders. Thus, when a government either violates the human rights of those subject to its authority or neglects to protect them against violations of human rights, the international com-munity not only has a right but an obligation to intervene. The report has spurred rich debates between (1) those who view R2P as a crucial advance in human rights doctrine that addresses a long-standing tension between state sovereignty (i.e., the right of states to control absolutely what occurs within their own borders) and concepts of universally applicable human rights norms and laws, and (2) those who see it as a dangerous erosion of the limited international legal protections against interference and outright invasion that weaker countries in the global hierarchy of states have against stronger ones. On a different front, many scholars have called into question the actual applicability of R2P, citing such recent crises in, for exam-ple, Syria, Afghanistan, the Republic of South Sudan, the Central African Republic, the Democratic Republic of the Congo, the Nuba Mountains and Blue Nile State in Sudan (not to mention Darfur), and Myanmar. The implications of these debates for intervention against and prevention of genocide are quite significant.

Feierstein, Daniel. 2009. "Getting Things into Perspective." *Genocide Studies and Prevention* 4 (2): 155–60.

This thought-provoking article is part of a set of critical evaluations of *Preventing Genocide: A Blueprint for US Policymakers*, often referred to as the Albright-Cohen Report. In it, Feierstein raises a crucial challenge to *Preventing Genocide*, its presumption that the United States (and, by extension, other great powers of the Global North) has a right to intervene (even without UN approval) in the internal affairs of other countries (which in practice mean weaker countries of the Global South) in order to enforce the UNCG. The author points out how the United States has intervened historically in many countries with dubious motives and negative consequences. The Albright-Cohen Report could rationalize further intervention, in contravention of "the national sovereignty of other states and even over international agreements" (155). Through his analysis, Feierstein highlights how the UNCG could be used for oppressive purposes.

Hallett, Nicole. 2009. "The Evolution of Gender Crimes in International Law." In *Plight and Fate of Women during and following Genocide*. Volume 7 of *Genocide: A Critical Bibliographic Review*, edited by Samuel Totten, 183–203. New Brunswick, NJ: Transaction Publishers.

This chapter traces the evolution of the treatment of rape and other gender crimes in international law and legal practice from the time of Grotius through 2008. It carefully examines the use of the UNCG in the prosecution of gender crimes, principally the recent concept of viewing rape in the context of genocide and as a tool of genocide. It is useful in highlighting the different aspects or functions of rape as they relate to international law, particularly the ICTR and ICTY, as well as some of the key debates regarding the relationship of rape and genocide today, such as whether considering "genocidal rape as a separate crime" (194) undermines recognition of rape itself as a general problem. The chapter recognizes that advances have ended "the days of absolute impunity for perpetrators of gender crimes" (196), though these advances have not been very effective in preventing mass gender crimes.

Human Rights Watch. 2004. *Genocide, War Crimes and Crimes against Humanity: Topical Digests of the Case Law of the International Criminal Tribunal for Rwanda and the International Criminal Tribunal for the Former Yugoslavia*. New York: Human Rights Watch. 482 pp.

This highly useful publication addresses a variety of issues regarding crimes against humanity, war crimes, and genocide, and presents short explanations of how and in what documents the ICTY and ICTR addressed them. It is a great tool for readers who want to go into further depth vis-à-vis court decisions and other documents regarding issues germane to genocide.

Kuper, Leo. 1981. *Genocide: Its Political Use in the Twentieth Century*. New Haven, CT: Yale University Press. 255 pp.

Genocide is an early, significant, and foundational book in the development of the field of genocide studies. Chapter 2 (pages 19–39) presents a comprehensive account of the drafting process of the UNCG that exposes the ways in which it resulted more from political deal-making and expediency than from a genuine intellectual and ethical analysis of genocide and what was needed to prevent it. The account highlights some of the exclusions made in the process, such as "political groups." Although Kuper presents ample reasons for seeing the UNCG as flawed and states that he does not necessarily agree that it contains a good definition of genocide, he asserts that both the UNCG and its definition of genocide should still be made use of because they are recognized internationally and thus can be a basis of action against genocide.

MacKinnon, Catharine A. 2006. *Are Women Human? And Other International Dialogues.* Cambridge, MA: Harvard University Press/Belknap Press. 419 pp.

Catharine MacKinnon is one of the world's leading theorists of gender and law, and had a major role in the creation of the concept of "sexual harassment" and its legal prohibition. In the 1990s, she played an active role in raising awareness regarding rape in Bosnia as an international legal problem and contributed to legal responses to it. In this book, she addresses a range of key gender and human rights issues to show that under the law and in practice women do not actually have proper human rights. Regarding genocide and the UNCG, MacKinnon explains why sexualized violence was not explicitly included in the UNCG and how understanding of such has evolved to the point at which rape is recognized as an act of genocide when committed under certain circumstances. She takes the position that, while, "on many levels, rape is rape ... genocidal rape can be distinguished ... from rape in war" and other contexts (221). At the same time, she raises a key issue: the reason that "rape, prostitution, forced pregnancy, forced and precluded abortion ... and pornography" (225) are effective tools of genocide is that they are already effective tools against women in everyday, non-genocidal life. Thus, "genocidal rape" in its destructive result on women is perhaps not fundamentally different from "everyday rape." Ultimately, MacKinnon raises important issues for anyone considering the intersection of gender and genocide, including in connection to the UNCG.

Mayersen, Deborah, ed. 2016. *The United Nations and Genocide.* London: Palgrave Macmillan. 262 pp.

The United Nations and Genocide analyzes how the UN has both met and failed to meet the commitment "to prevent and punish" the crime of genocide as spelled out in the UNCG. In doing so, the contributing authors discuss and analyze why the UN failed to effectively respond to a host of genocides, including those in Cambodia (1975–79), Rwanda (April–July 1994), the Balkans (the 1990s), and Darfur (2003–). Various authors also consider "new approaches recently adopted by the UN to address genocide."

Roscini, Marco. 2014. "Establishing State Responsibility for Historical Injustices: The Armenian Case." *International Criminal Law Review* 14 (2): 291–316.

Using the 1915 Armenian genocide as a focus, this article argues that the UNCG cannot be applied as law to cases of genocide occurring before it came into force. The argument turns on multiple points, including the absence of an explicit statement in the UNCG that it can be applied to cases before its entry into force; that application to a state for state responsibility is different from retroactive application to individuals, such as in the Nuremberg Trials and Eichmann Trial; and that UNCG did not merely codify laws already existing during the time of the Armenian genocide but created new law. Roscini's position contrasts with that developed by Alfred de Zayas in *Resolution with Justice: The Report of the Armenian Genocide Reparations Study Group* (Theriault et al. 2015). Importantly, Roscini's position accords with and anticipates the ICJ's 3 February 2015 judgment in the *Application of the Convention on the Prevention and Punishment of the Crime of Genocide* (*Croatia v. Serbia*), which establishes the impermissibility of retroactive legal application of the UNCG.

Sands, Philippe. 2016. *East West Street: On the Origins of "Genocide" and "Crimes against Humanity."* New York: Knopf. 448 pp.

Written by an international lawyer and professor of law at University College London, this book presents the highly engaging story of the development of the concepts of "crimes against humanity" and "genocide." It relates the stories of two men—Hersch Lauterpacht and Raphael Lemkin—both of whom were from the same town in Poland, whose immediate and extended families were caught in the maw of Nazi onslaught, and who were experts in the field of international law but held vastly different takes on what was needed to protect humanity from atrocity crimes. While Lauterpacht lobbied for an approach that focused on individuals (thus giving specific meaning to the term "crimes against humanity"), Lemkin lobbied for an approach that focused on groups (thus coining the term "genocide").

This is a key read for those interested in topics such as the protection of international human rights, the development of the international human rights regime, key distinctions between crimes against humanity and genocide, and the radical evolution of international law in the post–World War II world and the many and astounding ramifications of such.

Sewall, Sarah, Dwight Raymond, and Sally Chin. 2010. *Mass Atrocity Response Operations: A Military Planning Handbook.* Cambridge, MA: Harvard Kennedy School/Carr Center for Human Rights Policy. 156 pp.

This work lays out a comprehensive process for humanitarian military intervention operations. It looks at a range of challenges for such operations, from practical to political considerations, and attempts to formulate workable responses to them. The Spring 2011 issue of *Genocide Studies and Prevention* (volume 6, issue 1) contains a set of critical commentaries on the handbook that point out some of its flaws and problems.

Sjoberg, Laura. 2014. *Gender, War, and Conflict.* Cambridge, UK: Polity. 202 pp.

While this book deals only in a limited way explicitly with genocide, it is a good introduction to the increasingly prominent approach of considering international security, war, and human rights with attention to gender or "through a gendered lens," led first and foremost by Cynthia Enloe. In this way, it could be used as a good companion to *The United Nations Convention on the Prevention and Punishment of the Crime of Genocide: An Introduction.*

Theriault, Henry C. 2010. "Genocidal Mutation and the Challenge of Definition." *Metaphilosophy* 41 (4): 481–524.

In this article, Theriault argues that applications of the UNCG to past (as a justice mechanism), present (as an intervention tool), and potential genocides (as a deterrent) are undermined by the fixed definitional approach of the UNCG. Because genocide itself, as a practice that is developed by human beings, is always changing, the definition of genocide needs to keep up. Only by using a definition that evolves with changes can the promise of justice, intervention, and prevention made by the UNCG be fulfilled. Among other claims is that increased awareness of international law regarding genocide and human rights violations today has caused some perpetrators to choose methods of accomplishing genocide that do not quite fit—or that they believe do not quite fit—the UNCG, resulting in a situation in which the UNCG is perverted into a tool for attempting to avoid interference from the outside and future prosecution. Thus, Theriault argues, the evolution of genocide itself is in part the result of increasing awareness of the laws against and legal decisions regarding genocide as perpetrators try to stay ahead of the law.

Theriault, Henry C., Alfred de Zayas, Jermaine O. McCalpin, and Ara Papian. 2015. *Resolution with Justice: Reparations for the Armenian Genocide—The Report of the Armenian Genocide Reparations Study Group.* http://www.armeniangenocide - reparations.info/wp-content/uploads/2015/03/20150331-ArmenianGenocide -Reparations-CompleteBooklet-FINAL.pdf
    In this report, Alfred de Zayas (a renowned international law scholar and retired senior lawyer with the United Nations High Commissioner for Human Rights) presents a detailed analysis as to whether the UNCG can be applied to a genocide that occurred prior to its entry into force. De Zayas argues that it can be, based on his view that the UNCG is properly understood as supersessionary law—that is, a type of law that codifies previously existing international norms, principles, and agreements. He argues that the Armenian genocide was clearly illegal under international law (such as the 1899 and 1907 Hague Conventions) at the time of its commission, and that, with the updating of relevant international law via the UNCG, the UNCG could be applied to it. De Zayas's position contrasts with that of Marco Roscini in "Establishing State Responsibility for Historical Injustices: The Armenian Case," and with the ICJ's 3 February 2015 judgment in the *Application of the Convention on the Prevention and Punishment of the Crime of Genocide (Croatia v. Serbia)*, which establishes the impermissibility of retroactive legal application of the UNCG.

Totten, Samuel, ed. 2013. *Impediments to the Prevention and Intervention of Genocide.* Volume 9 of *Genocide: A Critical Bibliographic Review.* New Brunswick, NJ: Transaction Publishers. 304 pp.
    One chapter in particular, Samuel Totten's chapter 4, "The Wording and Interpretation of the UN Convention on the Prevention and Punishment of the Crime of Genocide: An Ongoing Impediment" (77–112), deals specifically with the UNCG.

— ed. 2017. *Last Lectures on the Prevention and Intervention of Genocide.* London: Routledge. 348 pp.

This book is comprised of over thirty "last lectures" by noted scholars of genocide studies, international relations, and international human rights. Each author was asked to project ahead and consider what he/she/they would want (or *need*) to say should he/she/they present his/her/their very last lecture on genocide. The authors were informed that they were welcome to take any angle, to be as controversial as they wanted, and to be as passionate as they wished. The array of positions, ideas, suggestions, and tone of the pieces is nothing short of remarkable. Among some of the many contributors to the book are Michael Barnett, Edina Bećirević, Israel Charny, Maureen Hiebert, Deborah Mayer, William Schabas, Gregory Stanton, Henry Theriault, Samuel Totten, and Johanna Vollhardt.

Works by Raphael Lemkin

Frieze, Donna-Lee, ed. 2013. *Totally Unofficial: The Autobiography of Raphael Lemkin*. New Haven, CT: Yale University Press. 328 pp.

This book presents the never-before-published autobiography of Raphael Lemkin. Reviewing this book in *The New Republic*, Michael Ignatieff wrote, in part, the following: "If the history of the Western moral imagination is the story of an enduring and unending revolt against human cruelty, there are few more consequential figures than Raphael Lemkin—and few whose achievements have been more ignored by the general public." This book presents a vivid account of the remarkable man who coined the term "genocide" and who was instrumental in the development of the UNCG.

Lemkin, Raphael. 1944. *Axis Rule in Occupied Europe: Laws of Occupation—Analysis of Government—Proposals for Redress*. Washington, DC: Carnegie Endowment for International Peace. 670 pp.

In 1943 Lemkin coined the word "genocide." When Lemkin's *Axis Rule in Occupied Europe* was published in November 1944, it was the first time the word "genocide" appeared in print. It was used in his discussion of Nazi Germany's occupation in Europe. Chapter 9 is entitled "Genocide." Lemkin's theorization of genocide in that chapter remains rich and important. It is essential reading for those studying genocide.

— 1945. "Genocide—A Modern Crime." *Free World* 9 (4): 39–43.

A general piece that provides an overview/summary of the concepts and proposals Lemkin delineated in chapter 9, "Genocide," of *Axis Rule in Occupied Europe*. *Free World* was a "non-partisan magazine devoted to the United Nations and Democracy" published during World War II.

— 1946. "Genocide." *American Scholar* 15 (2): 227–30. www.preventgenocide .org/lemkin/americanscholar1946.htm

An early discussion concerning the term and concept of genocide by Lemkin. It is comprised of the following sections: "A Crime without a Name," "The Word 'Genocide,'" "An International Crime," "Creating a Legal Framework," "Genocide in Time of War," and "Proposal for an International Treaty, including the Following Principles." The principles include seven points of discussion: a definition of genocide, universal repression, extradition, states and their accountability, the critical need to revise the Hague Convention, and multilateral treaties and the critical need to include anti-genocide clauses in peace treaties signed between various Axis Nations which have perpetrated genocide during World War II.

— 1947. "Genocide as a Crime under International Law." *American Journal of International Law* 41 (1): 145–51.

This piece presents a legal analysis and commentary on the 11 December 1946 General Assembly Resolution regarding the effort to establish the crime of genocide in international law. In the introduction to this piece, Lemkin asserts that the murderous actions of Nazi Germany against groups of people had led to a profound reconsideration of international law. He asserts that "the question arose whether government can destroy with impunity its own citizens and whether such acts of destruction are domestic affairs or matters of international concern" (146). From there, Lemkin discusses six key issues, all germane, in one way or another, to the development of the UNCG: "The Term 'Genocide,'" "Nuremberg," "The UN General Assembly," "The Genocide Resolution in the Legal Committee," "The Right of Intervention, a Future International Treaty, and the Principle of Universal Jurisdiction," and "The Peace Treaties and Germany's Criminal Code."

— 2002. "Totally Unofficial Man." In *Pioneers of Genocide Studies*, edited by Samuel Totten and Steven Jacobs, 365–99. New Brunswick: Transaction Publishers.

This is a long excerpt from Lemkin's autobiography that was never published during his lifetime.

Works about Raphael Lemkin

Bieńczyk-Missala, Agnieszka, and Dębski, Sławomir, eds. 2010. *Rafał Lemkin—A Hero of Humankind*. Warsaw: The Polish Institute of International Affairs. 319 pp.

This volume is comprised of a number of interesting and highly informative pieces by various scholars on Lemkin and/or genocide, including his role in the development of the UNCG as well as the fits and starts in the development and ratification of the UNCG. Contributors are from the United States, England, Poland, and Germany, and include William Schabas and Samuel Totten.

Cooper, John. 2008. *Raphael Lemkin and the Struggle for the Genocide Convention*. London: Palgrave Macmillan. 338 pp.

Cooper examines Lemkin's life, concerns, passions, projects, and struggle to prod the international community to establish a convention for the prevention and punishment of genocide, as well as his legacy.

Elder, Tanya. 2005. "What You See before Your Eyes: Documenting Raphael Lemkin's Life by Exploring His Archival Papers, 1900–1959." Special issue, *Journal of Genocide Research* 7 (4): 469–99.

Elder comments that "the purpose of this article is to further expose Raphael Lemkin through the lens of his archival collections, to see what Lemkin saw before his eyes and was determined to make others see as well. While many professions would benefit from knowing more about Lemkin's archival papers, it is of prime importance that those involved in Genocide Studies know about them, so as to act as visionaries to expand on his work. It is hoped that this study will provide a road-map to his collections for that purpose."

The initial section of this piece provides a succinct biographical sketch of Lemkin and an overview of where various documents by Lemkin are located, in addition to who originally located them and when. The other sections are entitled: "Nuremberg Tribunals and Hitler," "Lake Success Resolution/Genocide Convention (Geneva and Paris)," "Lobbying and the US Committee for a Genocide Convention," "Defense [of the Convention]," "Human Rights Legislation," "We Charge Genocide," "Dissemination [of information on genocide by Lemkin]," "Research—History of Genocide," "Instruction [about genocide by Lemkin]," and "Totally Unofficial" (Lemkin's autobiography).

Irvin-Erickson, Douglas. 2016. *Raphael Lemkin and the Concept of Genocide.* Philadelphia: University of Pennsylvania Press. 336 pp.

Of this book by the director of the Genocide Prevention Program at George Mason University, the publisher reports that

> this intellectual biography of one of the twentieth century's most influential theorists and human rights figures sheds new light on the origins of the concept and word "genocide," contextualizing Lemkin's intellectual development in interwar Poland and exploring the evolving connection between his philosophical writings, juridical works, and politics over the following decades. The book presents Lemkin's childhood experience of anti-Jewish violence in imperial Russia, his youthful arguments to expand the laws of war to protect people from their own governments, his early scholarship on Soviet criminal law and nationalities violence, his work in the 1930s to advance a rights-based approach to international law, his efforts in the 1940s to outlaw genocide, and his forays in the 1950s into a social-scientific and historical study of genocide, which he left unfinished, and examines how the meaning of genocide changed over the decades and highlights the relevance of Lemkin's thought to our own time.

"New Approaches to Raphael Lemkin." 2010. Special issue, *Journal of Genocide Research* 15 (3).

This special issue is comprised of the following articles: "New Approaches to Raphael Lemkin," by Donna-Lee Frieze; "A 'Synchronized Attack': On Raphael Lemkin's Holistic Concept of Genocide," by Thomas M. Butcher; "Genocide, the 'Family of Mind' and the Romantic Signature of Raphael Lemkin," by Douglas Irvin-Erickson; "Unofficial Men, Efficient Civil Servants: Raphael Lemkin in the History of International Law," by Mira L. Siegelberg; and "Prosecuting Genocide before the Genocide Convention: Raphael Lemkin and the Nuremberg Trials, 1945–1949," by Hilary Earl.

Korey, William. 2001. *An Epitaph for Raphael Lemkin.* New York: Blaustein Institute for the Advancement of Human Rights. 152 pages.

This book constitutes an introduction to Lemkin's "role in the development of a major instrument of international law: the Genocide Convention. Almost all aspects of the monograph relate in one way or another to Lemkin's intensive involvement with the historic treaty."

Moses, A. Dirk. 2010. "Raphael Lemkin, Culture, and the Concept of Genocide." In *The Oxford Handbook of Genocide Studies*, edited by Donald Bloxham and A. Dirk Moses, 19–41. Oxford: Oxford University Press.

This chapter provides an analysis of Raphael Lemkin's concept of genocide and highlights elements that remain relevant today.

Schaller, Dominik J., and Jürgen Zimmer, eds. 2009. *The Origins of Genocide: Raphael Lemkin as a Historian of Mass Violence*. New York: Routledge.

Schaller and Zimmer note that "this book was published as a special issue of the *Journal of Genocide Research*" (7[4]). They go on to assert that "the contributions in this book offer for the first time a critical assessment not only of [Lemkin's] influence on international law but also an historical analysis of mass murders, showing the close connection between both."

The book is comprised of the following pieces: "Introduction: The Origins of Genocide—Raphael Lemkin as a Historian of Mass Violence," by Dominik J. Schaller and Jürgen Zimmer; "Raphael Lemkin and the International Debate on the Punishment of War Crimes (1919–1948)," by Daniel Marc Segesser and Myriam Gessler; "What You See before Your Eyes: Documenting Raphael Lemkin's Life by Exploring His Archival Papers, 1900–1959," by Tanya Elder; "Raphael Lemkin as Historian of Genocide in the Americas," by Michael A. McDonnell and A. Dirk Moses; "Raphael Lemkin's View of European Colonial Rule in Africa: Between Condemnation and Admiration," by Dominik J. Schaller; "Raphael Lemkin on the Holocaust," by Dan Stone; and "Hostage of Politics: Raphael Lemkin on 'Soviet Genocide,'" by Anton Weiss-Wendt.

Documents on the UNCG: US, British, and Russian Archives

Weiss-Wendt, Anton, ed. 2018. *Documents on the Genocide Conventions from the American, British, and Russian Archives*, Volumes 1–2. London: Bloomsbury Publishers. 688 pp.

The publisher reports the following about this two-volume work: "This document collection highlights the legal challenges, historical preconceptions, and political undercurrents that had informed the UN Genocide Convention, its form, contents, interpretation, and application. It includes documents from eleven repositories in the United States, the United Kingdom, and Russia.... The selected records span the Cold War period and reflect on specific issues relevant to the Genocide Convention, as established at the time by the parties concerned. The types of documents reproduced in the collection include interoffice correspondence, memorandums, whitepapers, guidelines for national delegations, commissioned reports, draft letters, telegrams, meeting minutes, official and unofficial inquiries, formal statements, and newspaper and journal articles. On a classification curve, the featured records range from unrestricted to top secret. Taken in the aggregate, the documents reproduced in this collection suggest primacy of politics over humanitarian and/or legal considerations in the UN Genocide Convention."

The USSR and the UNCG

Weiss-Wendt, Anton. 2017. *The Soviet Union and the Gutting of the UN Genocide Convention*. Critical Human Rights. Madison: University of Wisconsin Press. 400 pp.

Based on extensive archival research, "Anton Weiss-Wendt reveals in detail how the political aims of the superpowers rendered the Convention a weak instrument for addressing abuses against human rights. The Kremlin viewed the genocide treaty as a political document and feared repercussions. What the Soviets wanted most was to keep the subjugation of Eastern Europe and the vast system of forced labor camps out of the genocide discourse. The American Bar Association and Senate Committee on Foreign Relations, in turn, worried that the Convention contained vague formulations that could be used against the United States, especially in relation to the plight of African Americans. Sidelined in the heated discussions, Weiss-Wendt shows, were humanitarian concerns for preventing future genocides."

The UNCG: Analyses, Commentary, and Case Law

Abtahi, Hirad, and Philippa Webb. 2008. *The Genocide Convention: The Travaux Préparatoires*. 2 vols. Leiden, The Netherlands: Brill. 965 pp.

The publisher reports that this two-volume set "gathers together for the first time in a single publication the records of the multitude of meetings which, in the context of the newly established United Nations, led to the adoption of the Convention on the Prevention and Punishment of the Crime of Genocide on 9 December 1948. This work will enable academics and practitioners easy access to the Genocide Convention's *travaux préparatoires*—an endeavour that has until now proven extremely difficult." Of this book, genocide scholar William Schabas wrote the following: "This accurate compilation of the *travaux préparatoires* of the Genocide Convention, with its indispensable index, will make the legal and philosophical debates that generated the text accessible to a much wider audience of students and practitioners."

Akhavan, Payam. 2012. *Reducing Genocide to Law: Definition, Meaning and the Ultimate Crime*. Cambridge: Cambridge University Press.

Written by a former prosecutor with the International Criminal Tribunal for the Former Yugoslavia, this highly acclaimed book raises a host of critical issues regarding the value of the UNCG itself. It is comprised of the following chapters: "The Power of a Word," "The Taxonomy of Crimes," "The Core Elements of International Crimes," "A Hierarchy of International Crimes," "Naming the Nameless Crime," "Who Owns Genocide?," "Contesting Genocide in Jurisprudence," and "Silence, Empathy, and the Potentialities of Jurisprudence." Of this book Luis Moreno Ocampo, the former Chief Prosecutor of the International Criminal Court, said: "Provokes a profound re-thinking of efforts to transform global aspirations into a reality." Martha Minow, the Dean of Harvard University Law School, wrote: "It is rare to have in one place the legal analysis of a scholar, the honest reportage of an eye-witness to history, and the humane reflections of an introspective soul."

Alonzo-Maizlish, David. 2002. "In Whole or In Part: Group Rights, the Intent Element of Genocide, and the 'Quantitative Criterion.'" *New York University Law Review* 77: 1369–1403.
An outstanding article that provides a host of valuable insights into the thorny issue of "in whole or in part" and the so-called "quantitative criterion" (i.e., whether the number of dead should influence the decision as to whether an event constitutes genocide or not).

Fein, Helen. 1992. *Genocide: A Sociological Perspective.* London: Sage Publications. 144 pp.
In this book, Helen Fein, a sociologist and scholar of genocide studies, provides a detailed and original discussion of the concept and history of genocide. In doing so, she examines the complicated issues of definition, causation, and the prevention of genocide. It is an excellent resource for professors and students alike to begin to understand the debates around the definition of genocide as the UNCG was being written in the late 1940s, as well as the ongoing debates in the 1980s and early 1990s as one scholar after another proffered his/her/their own definition of genocide. Fein's criticism of the latter is particularly interesting and informative.

Fournet, Caroline. 2016. *The Crime of Destruction and the Law of Genocide: Their Impact on Collective Memory.* London: Routledge. 218 pp.
The author examines the law relating to genocide, and explores the apparent failure of society to provide an adequate response to incidences of mass atrocity. Fournet's study illustrates the shortcomings of the Genocide Convention as a means of preventing and punishing genocide.

Gaeta, Paola, ed. 2009. *The UN Genocide Convention: A Commentary.* New York: Oxford University Press. 600 pp.
This edited book presents an analysis of the UNCG by "drawing on the Convention's *travaux préparatoires* [French for 'preparatory works,' in the plural; in legalese, it refers to the official record of a negotiation] and subsequent developments in international law." Written by highly respected international experts on the topic, the various chapters in the book present an analysis of each Article of the UNCG, "drawing on preparatory works and national and international case law." The book is divided into six parts: "Introduction," "The Crime of Genocide," "Repressing Genocide through Criminal Law," "Enforcing the Convention," "The Mechanics of the Convention," and "Taking Stock and Looking to the Future: The Convention in the XXIst Century."
Goldsmith, Katherine. 2010. "The Issue of Intent in the Genocide Convention and Its Effect on the Prevention and Punishment of the Crime of Genocide: Toward a Knowledge-Based Approach." *Genocide Studies and Prevention: An International Journal* 5 (3): 238–57.

The abstract to this article states the following:

Since the Genocide Convention was created in 1948, its effectiveness has been hindered by debates on what the definition actually means. It has been widely accepted that the meaning of "intent," within the Genocide Convention, refers to specific or special intent, *dolus specialis*. However, as more trials have taken place, creating more understanding of the crime of genocide, the linking of *dolus specialis* with the intent definition, that was so easily accepted at the first genocide trial (Akayesu at the International Criminal Tribunal for Rwanda [ICTR]), has been repeatedly put into question. The new approach being put forward as the most appropriate interpretation of "intent" is the knowledge-based approach. The Vienna Convention on Treaties states that interpretations of laws should follow the treaty's original purpose and objective, and should do this by looking at the preparatory work and its circumstances. By looking at the Travaux Préparatoires of the Genocide Convention and Raphael Lemkin's original writings on the subject, this article will discuss which approach fits the original intentions of both the drafters of the Convention and Lemkin himself, to determine which interpretation should be used in the future when considering the crime of genocide.

Lang, Berel. 2016. *Genocide: The Act as Idea*. Philadelphia: University of Pennsylvania Press. 176 pp.

In *Genocide: The Act as Idea*, Lang presents an analysis of the concept of genocide, discussing its strengths and weaknesses and how the latter can be ameliorated. In doing so, Lang "explores the relation of genocide to group identity, individual and corporate moral responsibility, the concept of individual and group intentions, and the concept of evil more generally." He makes the argument, which many may contest, that the concept of genocide constitutes "a notable advance in the history of political and ethical thought which proposed alternatives to it, like 'crimes against humanity,' fail to take into account."

Lingaas, Carola. 2015. "Defining the Protected Groups of Genocide through the Case Law of International Courts." ICD Brief 18. The Hague: International Crimes Database. 18 pp.

In the introduction to this article, the author states the following:

In defining the four protected groups of genocide, the international criminal tribunals have gradually shifted from an objective to a subjective approach, or a combination of these approaches with an emphasis on the subjective approach. The group membership is accordingly not determined by means of dubious objective parameters such as skin color, but by the perception of the group's differentness. Predominately, the courts determine the perpetrator's perception of the group that he wishes to single out and destroy. The Genocide Convention, however, exclusively protects four groups and a broadening of this protection to include any group created by the imagination of the perpetrator has consistently been rejected. The perpetrator's perception has therefore to be limited to what he understands to be a racial, national, ethnical or religious group. This analysis is primarily based on the case law of the international criminal courts, in particular the *ad hoc* tribunals for Rwanda and the Former Yugoslavia. It considers furthermore the case law of the International Criminal Court, the International Court of Justice and also includes the findings of the Darfur Commission.

Murray, Alexander R.J. 2011. "Does International Criminal Law Still Require a 'Crime of Crimes'? A Comparative Review of Genocide and Crimes against Humanity." *Goettingen Journal of International Law* 3 (2): 589–615.

Herein, the author argues that the crime of genocide "is now a redundant crime in international law given the advances that have been made in the case law and application of crimes against humanity." In doing so, he presents an historical analysis of each of the crimes, and then proceeds to "consider four separate crimes against humanity and corresponding acts of genocide." A key argument of the author concerns the "difficulties that stem from proving the intent in the mind of the perpetrator to destroy a particular group in contrast to the less demanding category of crimes against humanity."

Roger, Shayna. 2016. "Sexual Violence or Rape as a Constituent Act of Genocide: Lessons from the Ad Hoc Tribunals and a Prescription for the International Criminal Court." *George Washington International Law Review* 48 (2): 265–314.

The author notes that "Part I of this Article articulates the definition of genocide under international law, while Part II explains how sexual violence might function as an act of genocide pursuant to that definition. Parts III and IV explore the jurisprudence of the ICTR and ICTY, respectively, and discuss the extent to which each tribunal has prosecuted sexual violence as an act of genocide. Part V analyzes the progression (or lack thereof) of rape-as-genocide in the ICC, and Part VI contains a prescription for future ICC sexual violence prosecutions."

Schabas, William A. 2000. *Genocide in International Law*. Cambridge: Cambridge University Press. 624 pp.

Written by the noted scholar of international law and specialist on genocide William A. Schabas, this is an outstanding, clearly written, and highly detailed work on all aspects of genocide in international law. Schabas presents a thorough discussion of the UNCG, including the negotiations that led to the development of the UNCG and a detailed and enlightening discussion of the substantive areas of the UNCG. Highly recommended.

— 2006. "The 'Odious Scourge': Evolving Interpretations of the Crime of Genocide." *Genocide Studies and Prevention* 1 (2): 93–106.

In this article, Schabas analyzes court decisions on genocide to argue that the UN definition of genocide is evolving through its interpretation in case law, and that this evolution is sufficient to address concerns raised about the UN definition. To the extent that Schabas's analysis is correct, it displays important flexibility in both the UNCG and legal institutions in engaging genocide.

— 2010. "Retroactive Application of the Genocide Convention." *University of St Thomas Journal of Law and Public Policy* 4 (2): 36–59.

Schabas addresses two questions: (1) Does the Genocide Convention apply to acts or events prior to its entry into force? and (2) Did the crime of genocide exist under international law prior to 11 January 1951? Schabas concludes that, "although the hypothesis of retroactive operation of the Genocide Convention should not be totally dismissed, the prevailing view would seem to make this an unlikely scenario," and "there is very good authority for the proposition that genocide was a punishable crime under international law before the adoption of Resolution 96(I) and even before 1944, when the word itself was coined. There is an arguable case that the crime of genocide existed even before the Second World War, and as far back as 1914, although the authority becomes less and less solid the further back one goes. Certainly, there have been no prosecutions for pre-Second World War events. In any case, the issue is rather theoretical: because of the lapse of time, there are no known suspects alive who can be traced to acts perpetrated in 1915."

Sharlach, Lisa. 2010. "Rape as Genocide: Bangladesh, the Former Yugoslavia, and Rwanda." *New Political Science* 22 (1): 89–102.

In her introduction, Sharlach states the following:

> According to the 1948 Convention on the Prevention and Punishment of the Crime of Genocide, causing serious bodily or mental harm to members of an ethnic, national, religious and/or racial group and/or "deliberately inflicting on the group conditions of life calculated to bring about its physical destruction in whole or in part" constitute genocide. Rape certainly may cause serious physical and/or mental injury to the survivor, and also may destroy the morale of her family and ethnic community. However, this Convention does not explicitly state that sexual violence is a crime of genocide. The Convention should be expanded to include mass rape, regardless of whether the victims are raped on the basis of racial/ethnic, national, or religious identity. (89)

Tams, Christian, Lars Berster, and Bjorn Schiffbauer. 2014. *Convention on the Prevention and Punishment of the Crime of Genocide: A Commentary.* Oxford: Hart Publishing. 400 pp.

The authors present an article-by-article analysis of the 19 provisions of the UNCG. In doing so, they refer to case law and state practice. The book concludes with copies of the various versions of the treaty that were drafted between 1946 and 1948, a short history of the drafting process, and the definitions of genocide found in the national legislation of those states that have ratified the UNCG.

Van Der Wilt, H.G., Harmen Van der Wilt, and Jeroen Vervliet. 2012. *The Genocide Convention: The Legacy of 60 Years.* Leiden, The Netherlands: Martinus Nijhoff Publishers. 290 pp.

In their introduction, the authors state:

> Genocide is widely acknowledged as the crime of crimes. Such universal condemnation understandably triggers both loose talk (calling each and every massacre

genocide) and utter reluctance in political circles to use the G-word. The social construction of genocide reflects the deeper question whether the rigid legal concept of genocide as it emerges in the Genocide Convention and has been maintained ever since still corresponds with the historical and social perception of the phenomenon. This book is the product of an intellectual encounter between scholars of historical and legal disciplines that have joined forces to address this question. The authors are strongly inspired by the idea that the multi-disciplinary research of and education on genocide may contribute to a more appropriate reaction and prevention of genocide.

Van Schaack, Beth. 1996–97. "The Crime of Political Genocide: Repairing the Genocide Convention's Blind Spot." *Yale Law Journal* 106: 2259–91.

In her introduction to this "Note," Van Schaack, a professor of law at Santa Clara University School of Law, argues as follows:

> After protracted debate, the drafters of the Genocide Convention expressly excluded "political groups" from Article II. An examination of the *travaux préparatoires* of the Convention reveals the compromises born of politics and the desire to insulate political leaders from scrutiny and liability that can occur when political bodies attempt to reduce customary law principles to positivistic expression.... No legal principle can justify this blind spot. In this Note, I argue that the Genocide Convention is not the sole authority on the crime of genocide. Rather, a higher law exists: The prohibition of genocide represents the paradigmatic *jus cogens* norm, customary and peremptory norm of international law from which no derogation is permitted. The *jus cogens* prohibition of genocide, as expressed in a variety of sources, is broader than the Convention's prohibition, as has been demonstrated with respect to the jurisdictional principle applied to acts of genocide. Notwithstanding that the framers of the Genocide Convention attempted to limit the prohibition of genocide by deliberately excluding political groups from Article II, this provision is without legal force to the extent that it is inconsistent with the *jus cogens* prohibition of genocide.

United Nations Documents and Reports

UN Economic and Social Council, Commission on Human Rights, Sub-Commission on Prevention of Discrimination and Protection of Minorities. 1978. *Study of the Question of the Prevention and Punishment of the Crime of Genocide: Study Prepared by Mr. Nicodème Ruhashyankiko, Special Rapporteur.* 4 July. UN Doc. E/CN.4/Sub.2/416. New York: United Nations.

This is the first of two key reports commissioned by the United Nations since passage of the UNCG. It presents a comprehensive study of the UNCG, and addresses such issues as the exclusion of political groups, and what portion of a group "must be destroyed before an act committed with *that* end in view can be termed genocide" (14), the importance of "intent" in the definition of genocide, the possibility of the creation of an international criminal court two decades before the establishment of the ICC, and much more. The study is an indispensable compendium of information about the drafting of the Convention, including the fault lines and debates of the drafters and conceptual and practical issues.

— 1985. *Review of Further Developments in Fields with Which the Sub-Commission Has Been Concerned: Revised and Updated Report on the Question of the Prevention and Punishment of the Crime of Genocide: Prepared by Mr. B. Whitaker.* 2 July. UN Doc. E/CN.4/Sub.2/1985/6. New York: United Nations.

This second report commissioned by the United Nations on genocide and the UNCG adds important dimensions to the Ruhashyankiko report (see above). Among these are identification of cases of genocide that have been denied, such as the Armenians of the Ottoman Turkish Empire and the Aché of Paraguay; recognition that the perpetrators of a genocide might target their own group, as in the case of Cambodia; a recommendation to extend the groups protected to include "sexual group[s] such as women, men, [and] homosexuals" (16); the exclusion of "cultural genocide," "ethnocide," and "ecocide"; and concern about the challenges of enforcing the UNCG. This insightful and progressive look at genocide and the UNCG remains essential reading for those studying the UNCG as well as genocide more generally.

UN Secretariat. 1947. *Secretariat Draft (First Draft) of the Genocide Convention.* May. UN Doc. E/447. New York: United Nations.

This draft differs significantly from the final form of the UNCG. Of special note is its inclusion of "political" groups as well as "linguistic" groups among the types of group that can be targeted for genocide. Just as importantly, one category of genocide it presents is "cultural." These elements were all removed before the final version was approved. Examining these differences and others in light of background material on the dynamics of the drafting process, as presented in Kuper (see above), can help readers comprehend the complex development of the UNCG and appreciate the specific exclusions and inclusions that have become enshrined as international law.

UN General Assembly. 1948. *Convention on the Prevention and Punishment of the Crime of Genocide.* 9 December. United Nations, Treaty Series, vol. 78, p. 277. New York: United Nations. https://treaties.un.org/Pages/ViewDetails.aspx?src=IND&mtdsg_no=IV-1&chapter=4&clang=_en

This webpage contains the updated UNCG, with all signatories listed as well as their declarations, understandings, and reservations. The reservations are especially important, because they state which part(s) of the UNCG a particular country has indicated it does not consider itself bound by. Many of the signatories, including the United States, state reservations. Other signatories could indicate objections to reservations, and these are included as well. The reservations together represent an important limitation on the UNCG.

The United States and the UNCG

LeBlanc, Lawrence J. 1991. *The United States and the Genocide Convention.* Durham, NC: Duke University Press. 303 pp.

A fascinating and highly informative study of the forty-year struggle vis-à-vis the ratification of the UNCG by the United States. LeBlanc analyzes the original crafting of the UNCG and the United States' positions at that time concerning key components of the various drafts of the UNCG; discusses the barriers to the US ratifying the UNCG over a forty-year period; and explains why, during his presidency, Ronald Reagan chose to push for the ratification of the UNCG and was successful in doing so. As the publisher notes, "Through careful analysis of the bitter debates over ratification, LeBlanc demonstrates that much of the opposition to the Convention sprang from fears that it would be used domestically as a tool by groups such as blacks and Native Americans who might hold the U.S. accountable for genocide in matters of race relations." LeBlanc also does a solid job of outlining and discussing the "conditions" (commonly known as the "Lugar-Helms-Hatch Sovereignty Package") set by Congress upon the US ratification of the UNCG, which, LeBlanc argues, "markedly weakened the Convention."

Finally, LeBlanc also addresses the strengths and weaknesses of how the international community made use of the UNCG during that same forty-year period, and does so by examining cases of genocides committed across the globe in the years following World War II.

Alternatives to the Term/Concept of "Genocide"

Scheffer, David. 2006. "Genocide and Atrocity Crimes." *Genocide Studies and Prevention: An International Journal* 1 (3): 229–50.
In his abstract, Scheffer states the following:

> The term "genocide" has been commonly used ... to describe atrocities of great diversity, magnitude, and character. Yet the prospect of the term's arising in policymaking too often imposes an intimidating brake on effective responses. The political use of the term should be separated from its legal definition.... Governments and international organizations should be liberated to apply the term "genocide" more readily ... to publicly describe precursors of genocide and react rapidly either to prevent or to stop mass killings or other seeming acts of genocide.... There also is a critical need for a new term—"atrocity crimes"—and a new field of international law—atrocity law—to achieve a similar objective, namely, to enable public and academic discourse to describe genocide, crimes against humanity (including ethnic cleansing), and war crimes with a single term that is easily understood by the public and accurately reflects the magnitude and character of the crimes.... The purpose would be to simplify and yet render more accurate both public dialogue and legal terminology describing genocide and other atrocity crimes.

Educational Resources

Facing History and Ourselves. 2007. *Totally Unofficial: Raphael Lemkin and the Genocide Convention*. https://www.facinghistory.org/books-borrowing/totally -unofficial-raphael-lemkin-and-genocide-convention. PDF download requires login

This booklet includes the following: a historical case study of Raphael Lemkin and his legacy, study questions, lesson plans using the case study, a list of primary source documents, and a list of other resources ideal for use in the classroom.

—— 2013. "Lesson 2 of 3: Exploring Raphael Lemkin's Actions: The Invention of the Word 'Genocide.'" *Totally Unofficial: Raphael Lemkin and the Genocide Convention: A Series of Three Lessons.* https://www.facinghistory.org/resource -library/totally-unofficial-raphael-lemkin-and-genocide/exploring-lemkins -actions-invention-word-genocide

The introduction to this lesson states the following: "This lesson focuses on how Lemkin turned his moral outrage into action.... Following Lemkin's path, students will explore the concept of sovereignty that made it difficult to pros- ecute perpetrators of genocide.... Lemkin took it upon himself to invent a new word—genocide—to represent acts committed with the intent to destroy a group of people. In this lesson, students will begin to understand Lemkin's notion of what genocide is, as they also consider their own definitions of crimes against humanity and civilization." This lesson draws on information from Readings 2, 3, and 5 in Facing History's *Totally Unofficial: Raphael Lemkin and the Genocide Convention* (see above).

In addition to the above "Overview," this lesson includes the following com- ponents: "Learning Goals (and Essential Questions)," "List of Materials Needed for the Lesson," a "List of Activities," and "Extensions." The lesson is said to take two class periods.

—— 2013. "Lesson 3 of 3: Continuing Lemkin's Legacy: What Can We Do to Prevent and Stop Genocide?" *Totally Unofficial: Raphael Lemkin and the Genocide Convention: A Series of Three Lessons.* https://www.facinghistory.org/resource -library/totally-unofficial-raphael-lemkin-and-genocide/continuing-lemkins -legacy-what-can-we-do-prevent-stop-genocide

This lesson, which draws on information from Readings 5 and 6 of the case study delineated in *Totally Unofficial: Raphael Lemkin and the Genocide Convention* (see above), focuses to a large extent on the UNCG. Two of the learning goals are for students to expand their knowledge of the United Nations Convention on the Prevention and Punishment of the Crime of Genocide and to understand the limits of the Genocide Convention in stopping and preventing genocide. One of its "Essential Questions" is, "If we have a Genocide Convention, why does genocide still happen?" The lesson includes "Warm-Up Activities" and "Comprehension Questions about the UNCG." While the main lesson focuses on the Darfur geno- cide, each of the aforementioned activities on the UNCG can be used as they are in the classroom without undertaking the entire lesson.

Patton, Larry. 1987. "An Interview with US Senator William Proxmire on US Ratification of the Genocide Convention." Special issue, *Social Science Record* 24 (2): 42–43.

This interview details Senator Proxmire's persistence, over nineteen years, to achieve Congressional ratification of the United Nations Genocide Convention. It explains his views on its strengths and weaknesses and his conviction that the topic of genocide should be included in the secondary curriculum. It stresses his support for the UNCG and assesses the then-current attempts to revise it.

International Criminal Tribunals and International Courts: Websites

International Criminal Court (ICC). https://www.icc-cpi.int/Pages/Main.aspx
The ICC is the international court devoted to "trying individuals for genocide, crimes against humanity, war crimes, and aggression." This official website of the ICC provides recent news from the court, background on the court and how it functions, as well as a host of downloadable documents related to the court, including reports on the ICC's activities, trial transcripts, and much more. Website visitors can even watch livestreams of ongoing cases.

International Court of Justice (ICJ). http://www.icj-cij.org/en
The ICJ is the United Nations court for cases between countries. It does not deal at all with individual issues, but instead is devoted to settling disputes between states. It is rare for a case of genocide to be heard by the court because all cases must be agreed to by both states, either at the time of submission or through some earlier agreement. Article IX of the UNCG means that those countries bound by the convention agree that any single party may bring a case to the ICJ. The court can also provide advisory legal opinions. The ICJ website contains information about how the court works and various documents, including case decisions and advisory opinions.

International Criminal Tribunal for Rwanda (ICTR). http://unictr.unmict.org/
The ICTR ended its work on 31 December 2015, but its website remains accessible. It contains background on the court and information on all its cases as well as the various legal documents from the cases, including judgments. Study of these documents provides readers with exceptional insight into the 1994 Rwandan Genocide, and the legal response to it. Application of the UNCG is prominent in the cases. This allows readers to analyze the ways that the UNCG was effective and where and why it was ineffective.

International Criminal Tribunal for the Former Yugoslavia (ICTY). http://www.icty.org/
The ICTY functioned until 2017. Similar to the ICTR website, the ICTY's website contains background information as well as a host of documents, including case judgments. Study of these documents provides readers with exceptional insight into the violence in the former Yugoslavia, and the legal response to it.

About the Authors

SAMUEL TOTTEN is Professor Emeritus at the University of Arkansas, Fayetteville (1987–2012). He has a doctorate from Columbia University in New York City. His areas of research are crimes against humanity and genocide in Sudan; the impact of genocide on the individual and the local community; and the intervention and prevention of genocide. He taught the first course on the history of genocide ever offered on the flagship campus of the University of Arkansas, Fayetteville in the Department of Political Science.

During the summer of 2004, Totten served as one of the 24 investigators with the US State Department's Atrocities Documentation Project (ADP), whose express purpose was to collect data in order to ascertain whether genocide had been perpetrated in Darfur by the Government of Sudan (GoS). The investigation was conducted in refugee camps along the Chad/Darfur Sudan border. The data collected by the ADP was ultimately used by US Secretary of State Colin Powell to declare, on 9 September 2004, that Sudan had perpetrated genocide in Darfur and possibly was still doing so. Subsequently, Totten and Eric Markusen, a genocide scholar and ADP investigator, produced a book about the ADP: *Genocide in Darfur: Investigating Atrocity in the Sudan* (Routledge, 2006).

In 2008, Totten served as a Fulbright Scholar at the Centre for Conflict Management at the National University of Rwanda. While there he conducted a study of the *gacaca* process (trials of alleged *genocidaires* by local courts), and completed a book with Rafiki Ubaldo entitled *We Cannot Forget: Interviews with Survivors of the 1994 Genocide in Rwanda* (Rutgers University Press, 2011).

For the past sixteen years Totten has conducted research into the Darfur Genocide (2003 to present) and the Nuba Mountains Genocide (late 1980s into the 1990s) in refugee camps along the Chad/Darfur border, and in the Nuba Mountains in Sudan. During the war between the Government of Sudan and the Sudan People's

Liberation Movement-North, Totten traveled to the Nuba Mountains on five different occasions and provided much-needed provisions on those trips to civilians who had been bombed off their farms by Government of Sudan aerial attacks. Based on this research, Totten wrote *Genocide by Attrition: Nuba Mountains, Sudan* (Transaction Publishers, 2013, with a revised second edition in 2015), and edited two other books, *Conflict in the Nuba Mountains: From Genocide by Attrition to the Current Crises* (Routledge, 2015) and *Sudan's Nuba Mountains People Under Siege: Accounts by Humanitarians from the Battle Zone* (McFarland Publishers, 2016).

Between 2005 and 2012, Totten served as one of the founding co-editors of *Genocide Studies and Prevention: An International Journal* (University of Toronto Press) and as the managing editor of Genocide: *A Critical Bibliographic Review* series for Transaction Publishers from 2000 to 2013. Among some of the many other books Totten has authored, co-authored, and co-edited on genocide are *Dictionary of Genocide* (Greenwood Publishers, 2008); *An Oral and Documentary History of the Darfur Genocide* (Praeger Security International, 2010); *Century of Genocide: Critical Essays and Eyewitness Accounts*, fourth edition (Routledge, 2013); *Last Lectures: The Prevention and Intervention of Genocide* (Routledge, 2018); and *Dirty Hands, Vicious Deeds: The US Government's Complicity in Genocide* (University of Toronto Press, 2018).

HENRY THERIAULT is currently Associate Vice President for Academic Affairs at Worcester State University in the United States, after teaching in its Philosophy Department from 1998 to 2017. From 1999 to 2007, he coordinated the University's Center for the Study of Human Rights.

Theriault's research focuses on genocide denial, genocide prevention, post-genocide victim-perpetrator relations, reparations, and mass violence against women and girls. Since 2007, he has chaired the Armenian Genocide Reparations Study Group and is lead author of its March 2015 final report, *Resolution with Justice*. He has published numerous journal articles and chapters, and edited or co-edited two books. In 2017, Theriault was elected President of the International Association of Genocide Scholars (IAGS), and has been re-elected in 2019.

He has lectured and given panel papers around the world, including in Armenia, Turkey, the Mountainous Karabakh Republic, Lebanon, Australia, Japan, South Korea, Rwanda, Britain, France, Belgium, Italy, Argentina, Canada, Cambodia, and across the United States. During the summer of 2013 he was a visiting scholar at the Australian National Research Council's Centre of Excellence in Policing and Security at Griffith University.

He is founding co-editor of the peer-reviewed *Genocide Studies International*. From 2007 to 2012 he served as co-editor of the International Association of Genocide Scholars's peer-reviewed *Genocide Studies and Prevention*, and has guest-edited for the *International Criminal Law Review* and the *Armenian Review*.

Index